THE
SEEDLING
QUILTS

11 ENGLISH PAPER PIECED AND
APPLIQUED DESIGNS INSPIRED
BY MEDICINAL HERBS

JODI GODFREY

TUVA PUBLISHING

www.tuvapublishing.com

Address

Merkez Mah. Cavusbasi Cad. No:71

Cekmekoy - Istanbul 34782 / Turkey

Tel: +9 0216 642 62 62

The Seedling Quilts

First Print

2019 / May

All Global Copyrights Belong To
Tuva Tekstil ve Yayıncılık Ltd.

Content
Quilting

Editor in Chief
Ayhan DEMİRPEHLİVAN

Project Editor
Kader DEMİRPEHLİVAN

Designer
Jodi GODFREY

Technical Editors
Leyla ARAS
Büşra ESER

Graphic Designers
Ömer ALP
Abdullah BAYRAKÇI
Zilal ÖNEL

Photograph
Jane McLean
Jodi Godfrey
Tuva Publishing

ISBN
978-605-9192-71-2

TuvaYayincilik TuvaPublishing
TuvaYayincilik TuvaPublishing

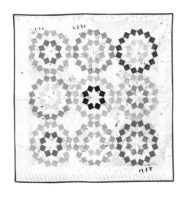

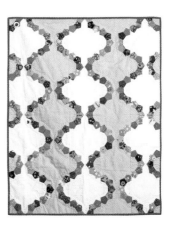

CONTENTS

INTRODUCTION 7

THE QUILTS IN THIS BOOK 8

TOOLS AND MATERIALS 10

HOW TO ENGLISH PAPER PIECE 16

HOW TO APPLIQUE EPP 20

HOW TO FINISH YOUR QUILT 22

QUILTS

MYRTLE 26

CARAWAY 38

PEPPERMINT 46

YARROW 52

HONEYSUCKLE 62

FEVERFEW 70

ELDERBERRY 76

CORNFLOWER 82

ROSEMARY 92

LAVENDER 98

SEEDLINGS QUILT 106

PROJECT GALLERY

26

38

52

46

106

70

76

82

62

98

92

INTRODUCTION

I have a deep admiration for a handful of women in my life who grow beautiful gardens. With persistence and skill and an incredible amount of hard work, they have created havens of shade and colour, of buzzing activity and refreshing quiet, of peace and joy. Unfortunately, as hard as I've tried over the years, I have not become one of them.

I first tried to grow a garden seriously when my oldest boy, Tully, was little. But I quickly realised that his happy following behind me, pulling plants out as quickly as I'd planted them, and washing my seeds away with the blast of his hose, was not going to be the blessed family project of which I had always dreamed. We sowed seeds that didn't grow, killed plants I'd spent good money on, and never, ever kept up with the weeds. There were already so many things in my life that died or turned to chaos if not regularly managed – the dishes, the laundry, the toddler – that I decided I wasn't quite ready to add a garden to the list. In the end, my yard became a hodge-podge of plants and trees that were happy just being left to themselves.

It was around this time that I started to dabble in quilting. Just slowly, and just here and there. It didn't take long for me to notice that this lovely craft, no matter how long it was left unattended, didn't undo itself, or become over-run with weeds.

It just waited. I could come back to it a few days, or a month, or even a year later, and it was there, ready for me to pick up where I left off. There was no pressure to do a little every day in order to keep on top of things. It just let me enjoy it as I was able. And when I finished a quilt, it was finished. Not like the dirty dishes that hit the bench the second you empty the sink and hang up your towel. It was done and ready to be included in our little family.

It was this realisation that got me hooked on making quilts.

The quilts in this book are a representation of the kind of garden I would love to grow, if I ever manage to pull it off! They are named for and inspired by flowers and shrubs that have been used for centuries for their beauty, symbolism, and healing properties. Flowers that enhance the taste of food or deter bugs, flowers that relieve pain and anxiety, flowers to mark celebrations and bereavement. I would love one day, to cultivate a garden that brings that kind of health and joy to my corner of the world, but for now, these 11 quilts are my garden. It is my sincerest hope that in making them also, you'll experience some of that health and joy!

To read more about the history and uses of the herbs in this book, head to: www.talesofcloth.com/seedlings

THE QUILTS IN THIS BOOK

This book includes 10 English Paper Pieced designs and 11 quilts. Seedlings, the inspiration quilt, is made up of panels of each of the designs in a medallion/log cabin format. Each chapter offers a pattern for both the Seedlings panel, and the stand-alone quilt inspired by it. You'll find the final instructions for sewing the Seedlings panels together in the last chapter.

For this book, I have played with different elements of quilt-making, mixing EPP with appliqué and machine piecing. Sometimes, while stitching the quilts, I discovered that mixing up the traditional order of things made the construction simpler, so I occasionally appliquéd pieces after basting the quilt

sandwich rather than before, or machine stitched them to a pieced quilt top. Be sure to read the instructions through first before starting your quilt to avoid unnecessary challenges!

All the quilts in this book were made from stash except for Lavender Quilt (fabric supplied by Art Gallery Fabrics) and Caraway Quilt (Fabric bought from Polka Dot Tea). I wanted to make sure these quilts felt a little timeless, and able to be made by anyone with a scrap collection. I hope they make you feel like you can dive right in!

All of the English paper pieces for these quilts can be purchased from shop.talesofcloth.com

TOOLS AND MATERIALS

FABRIC

I love to work with quilting weight cotton best, but I've also enjoyed EPP with lawn, linen, and even flannel! Because EPP parts are often small, and don't require exact seam allowances, scraps of all shapes and sizes are perfect for EPP. I tend to buy fat quarters for small prints and half yards for bigger designs that I might want to fussy cut.

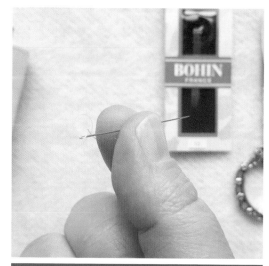

NEEDLES

I use Bohin Milliners size 9 for EPP and applique. And Bohin Crewel size 6 for big-stitch quilting. As needle size numbers go up, the smaller the needle becomes. If you find your needle too fine, try the number below, and if your needle is too thick, try a higher number. When I stitch, I want the eye to be easy to thread, and I don't want to have to yank the thread through the fabric after the needle.

IRON

Scraps are easier to work with after a quick press. But honestly, my iron mostly only comes out once my quilt top is finished, or to make binding. The iron is also handy for marking a crease in background fabric to use as a guide for placing appliqued shapes and blocks.

THREAD

I like to use Aurifil 50wt cotton thread. If you use cotton thread, be sure to thread the needle at the end that comes off the spool first. Cotton is directional, and stitching against the grain increases knotting and tangling. I generally just use whatever colour I have sitting closest to me, but I do have a particular fondness for Butter, Sand, Fog and Bari Variegated 4651. I used DMC Perle 8 for quilting. One day I dream of owning all the colours!

SCISSORS

I find myself using scissors a lot to cut fabric with EPP (rather than just a rotary cutter), so make sure yours are comfortable and sharp. I like my Ginghers.

Keep a small pair of snips on hand also for easy thread snipping and unpicking (I also have a quick unpick but can never find it for some reason!).

GLUE

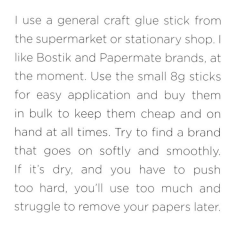

I use a general craft glue stick from the supermarket or stationary shop. I like Bostik and Papermate brands, at the moment. Use the small 8g sticks for easy application and buy them in bulk to keep them cheap and on hand at all times. Try to find a brand that goes on softly and smoothly. If it's dry, and you have to push too hard, you'll use too much and struggle to remove your papers later.

I use these glue sticks for basting the fabric to my paper shapes and for holding my applique in place. There are other, more craft-specific, glues on the market that work wonderfully, and often better, than glue sticks, but are generally several times the price and only available from quilt shops (a 30-minute drive for me rather than the few minutes into town).

PAPER

We use 100% recycled card and envelopes for our paper pieces and we don't use any plastic in our packaging. Tales of Cloth papers are easy to fold (essential for stitching around corners), laser cut for accuracy, and re-usable once or twice. If you're buying a disposable product, why not make it an earth-friendly one?

ACRYLIC TEMPLATES

I use acrylic templates for fussy cutting only, but many people use them for cutting every piece. If you're someone who likes to centre a design on the paper piece, or loves neat, consistent seams in your quilt, templates are for you. We cut ours with a ⅜" seam allowance because that makes it much easier to baste.

ROTARY CUTTER, RULER AND CUTTING MAT

Most of my cutting from stash is done by rotary cutting the right-sized strip from a piece of fabric, placing the shape on the strip, and cutting an approximate seam allowance around it. Some shapes fit nicely in a square or rectangle, and others can be flipped upside down to get good use of the strip. It's quick and easy when you want several pieces from the same fabric (like background fabric).

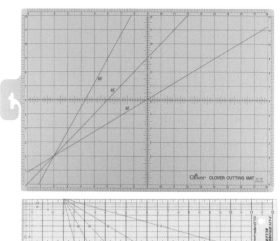

ZIP LOCK BAGS

I still have a huge collection of zip lock bags from my days of online quilting bees, and almost every one of them is in use today. Zip Lock bags are great for keeping a block's worth of basted shapes together so that you can travel with them, or simply remember the colour combination you chose.

PENS FOR MARKING

I use a ball point pen for marking around acrylic templates for fussy cutting. And I use a white board marker for marking around a design on the acrylic template so that I can locate the same part of the repeat again, accurately, for fussy cutting. The whiteboard marker wipes off easily with a tissue.

THIMBLE

I tend not to use a thimble because I push the needle away from me using my thumb, and my thumbnail holds the needle steady and stops my skin getting hurt. This, however, is a habit I picked up from teaching myself to stitch. If you hold your needle and stitch in a more traditional manner, you'll probably find a thimble useful. There are lots of different solutions available these days, from rubber thimbles with a metal top, to small stick-on pads that you can place anywhere on your fingers that tend to get tender.

SPRAY BASTE AND BASTING PINS

I use 101 or 501 brands of spray baste to baste my quilt sandwich ready for quilting. If my quilt is really big, I tend to use pins because it's easier to get a flat sandwich without all the getting up and down and moving layers that happens with gluing. For some reason, cotton lawn doesn't like glue, so I use pins when using a lawn backing.

CLOVER CLIPS

I use Clover Wonder Clips to hold small bundles of basted shapes together for stitching later, for 'pinning' long seams together so they don't slip while I'm stitching, and for marking sections of blocks that I want to keep open (this is especially useful if your blocks share joining shapes and you only want to stitch a few to each block). Clover clips are also essential for keeping your paper and fabric in place if you thread baste.

SEWING MACHINE

The patterns in this book only use straight stitch, and only use a sewing machine to attach borders, sew panels together, or attach binding. No fancy stitches or gadgets required, though you might appreciate your quarter inch foot if you have one.

BATTING / WADDING

I use 100% cotton or 80/20 cotton/poly blend for my quilts. My favourite is Legacy brand, which is often available by the bolt at Spotlight in Australia. I tend to just get whatever is on special though!

PAPER PIECES

HOW TO ENGLISH PAPER PIECE CUTTING

STRIP CUTTING

The method I use most for EPP, and that I refer to most often in my patterns, is cutting shapes from strips. Lay your paper template ⅜" from the bottom of your fabric. Using a ruler and rotary cutter, cut a strip ⅜" above the paper. Keep your paper shape at the left end of the fabric strip, ⅜" away from the edge. Rotary cut ⅜" away from the right side of the paper.

If your shape has its opposite edges running parallel (like diamonds, squares, or octagons), you can simply take another shape, and place it ⅜" away from the line you're just cut, and then cut again ⅜" on the right.

If your shape has opposite edges running towards each other (like triangles, jewels, or half hexagons), you can flip the template upside down after the first cut, and line it up ⅜" away from the cut line.

Shapes like hexagons and crowns don't tessellate neatly inside a strip, but I cut squares or rectangles for them anyway. You can trim the rectangle ⅜" around the paper shape if you like, but I tend to leave it.

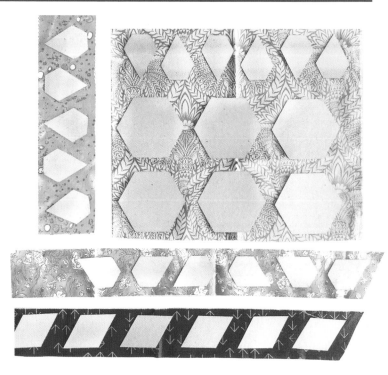

SCRAP CUTTING

If I just want a couple of pieces per print, for a really scrappy look, or if I'm digging around my scrap bucket, I tend to simply place the paper shape in a corner of the fabric and cut an approximate seam allowance around it with scissors.

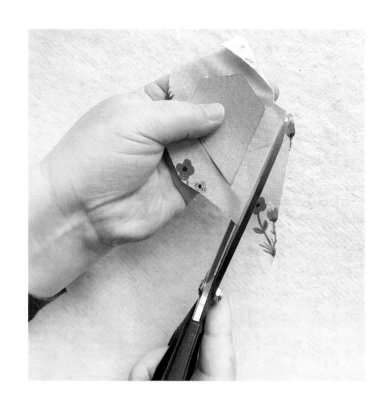

FUSSY CUTTING

I don't use fussy cutting as much as scrappy patchwork because I tend to be a flitty kind of quilter rather than a focused one, and fussy cutting requires a bit more time and concentration. The results, however, can be fantastic. Check your fabric first, that you have the right number of repeats in a cut. Find a flower or bird or something else easy to place, and then count how many of that exact same motif is in your fabric. If there's only 4, and you need 6, you're going to run into trouble. Medium-sized florals and geometric designs will give you the best chance of an effective fussy cut from a smaller cut of fabric.

Place your acrylic template over the motif you wish to repeat. Draw over the picture on the acrylic template with a whiteboard marker, so you can line it up exactly next time.

Now draw around the acrylic template with a ball point pen to mark your cutting line. (You can cut around the template with a rotary cutter, but I find this method less awkward, and easily done at the dining room table.) Being careful not to wipe off the whiteboard marker, line up the acrylic template with the same motif in another part of the fabric. Once you've drawn around your template the necessary times, cut out your fabric with scissors.

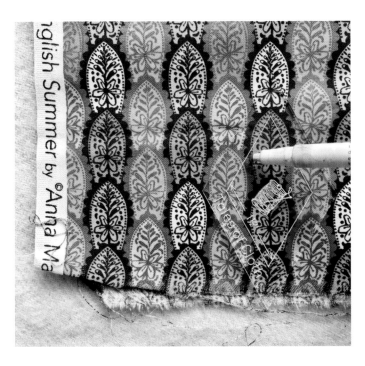

BASTING

GLUE BASTING

I use glue basting for all of my EPP. Centre the paper shape on the fabric and put a thin line of glue just inside the edge of the paper. Keeping the glue off the edge will make stitching easier later because your fold is not full of glue. Keep the paper and fabric still with one hand, and with the other, fold the fabric over the paper shape and press it flat. Turn the paper and fabric slightly to make the next edge easy to access, and glue. Fold the seam over the paper. Make your way around the paper until all sides are basted.

THREAD BASTING

People who prefer thread basting like it because it's less sticky and more portable than using glue. I like it less because I find it slower, and I don't mind basting in bulk at the dining table or on a hardcover book on my lap. Thread basting is handy for applique when you want to remove the papers easily and keep the fabric in shape. I also prefer it for basting tiny shapes (though I generally avoid tiny shapes!).

Centre the paper shape on the fabric. Fold one seam over the paper and hold it in place with a Clover Clip or paperclip. Now turn to the opposite side of the shape and fold the seam over the paper. Hold it in place between your left finger and thumb and fold the adjacent seam over also. Thread your needle through the fold of the fabrics in the corner and pull the thread until you have a small tail. Stitch through the same spot a couple of times to hold the thread in place. If your shape is small (an inch or so along the sides), you can fold the next seam over and stitch in the corner without going through the paper. This makes it easy to remove papers later and press your quilt top. If your shape is bigger, you'll need to stitch through the seam and paper template between corners, and then stitch back up through the paper at the next corner. To release the paper later, you'll need to snip the threads that hold it in place.

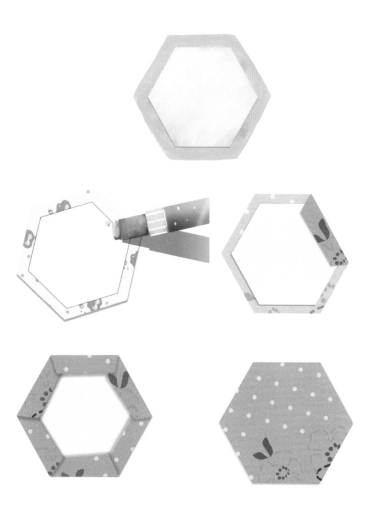

EPP KNOT

For EPP, I hold my paper shapes right sides together, thread through the corners for both shapes, catching the fabric only, and then I pull the thread through until I have a small tail. Stitch through the same point a couple more times, and in the final loop made by the fabric, thread the needle through twice and pull to knot it in place. I try to start and finish my thread in corners or at joining points but sometimes you can't avoid finishing half way through a seam. Knot in the same way to finish the thread.

STITCHING

After making a knot, keep your pieces held right sides together and whip stitch along the edge of the shapes, careful to just get the fabric. I stitch around 8-10 stitches per inch. If you don't like your stitches showing, look up 'invisible ladder stitch' or other invisible EPP stitches online. There are lots of good video tutorials out there. I don't mind seeing my stitches as practice has made them neat and small.

TRIMMING

If you are attaching borders or stitching your EPP panels to other fabric pieces, you'll need to trim your EPP to ¼" from where the papers have been. Line up your quilting ruler so that the quarter inch line meets up with the end of the stitching along the side of the panel. Use your rotary cutter to trim.

If your EPP edges haven't finished square and you need to make a straight edge, find the points of the EPP that are closest to the edge, but the furthest in from other points hanging over the edge. Measure a ¼" from those points and trim. For most of the patterns in this book, I have provided half shapes to make the edges square. In some cases, however, making square edges requires a lot more thought and decision making than is worth a little wasted fabric, and so I have kept the shapes as is.

When your trimming takes you through a seam, rather than just ¼" from a knot, you end up with loose seams. In these cases, I always make sure I trim right before I add my

PAPERS OUT AND PRESSING

While you don't need to press between seams, as with regular patchwork, you do need to give your work one big press at the end. If your quilt is made up of lots of tiny pieces in blocks, I recommend removing the papers that are completely surrounded in each block and giving it a press as you go. It'll make your job much easier at the end!

Once you have finished your quilt top, take the remaining papers out. Tiny diamonds are especially good at hiding, even when ironing, so try to move across your quilt in an orderly manner, completing a section at a time. Holding your patchwork up to the light will help you detect any last, hiding shapes. Unless the pattern instructs otherwise, you will generally press all of the inner seams in. The seams around the outside, that need their seam allowance for attaching borders or binding, will need to be pressed out and trimmed. Steam is your friend when pressing EPP!

MACHINE SEWING EPP PANELS

When adding borders or machine sewing panels together, I always have the EPP side on top so that I can direct the seams under the foot in the right direction, and line up the points perfectly with the needle. Before I switched to EPP, I always had the smaller piece on top to make it easy to move if needed, so it might take a little getting used to. Use pins to keep things in place. Any seams that are machine sewn in this book use a ¼" seam allowance.

borders and use pins to stop the seams from coming apart while attaching the borders with my machine.

If I'm not adding borders, I'll leave the trimming until after I've quilted, so that everything stays in place until I'm ready to bind.

HOW TO APPLIQUE EPP

APPLIQUE AND EPP

Some of the blocks and panels in this book are appliqued to a background rather than pieced to the edge. Sometimes the applique happens after a block is complete, and sometimes after a row of blocks are stitched together. Read through your patterns carefully so that you don't take your papers out too early.

Once your block/row is complete and ready to stitch to a background fabric, take all the papers out and press. If you are appliqueing your block in open space, you'll press all of your seams under the block. Don't worry about tails just yet. You can poke them in while stitching. If you're appliqueing your block to the edge of a background, and the fabric in the block is needed for seam allowance, you'll need to press that edge out and trim it to ¼"

APPLIQUE KNOT

For applique, thread the needle, and then take the end of the thread and bring it around to meet the point of the needle. Take the end of the thread in the finger and thumb that's holding your needle, and then with your other hand, wind the thread around the needle several times. Pull the needle though the winded thread all the way along until a knot forms at the end of the thread.

APPLIQUE STITCH

If block placement needs to be exact, fold your background fabric and press to create guidelines. Use glue or pins to hold your applique in place. (I prefer glue because it's less sharp than stitching around pins!) Begin in a corner if your block is in space, or at one side if your block is in line with the background fabric. Put your needle in from the back, through the background fabric and the edge of the block. Pull the thread through until it hits the knot. Put the needle back into the background fabric directly in line with the first hole. And then manoeuvre the needle to come back up through the background fabric and block about 1/16" from the last stitch. Pull the thread. Continue around the block. This should give you straight, tiny stitches around your block. Give the block another quick press once you're done

HOW TO FINISH YOUR QUILT

MAKING THE BACKING

For my quilt patterns, I've allowed enough fabric in the backing requirements to fold your backing fabric in half so that the fold runs from selvedge to selvedge. Cut along the fold and sew the pieces along one selvedge, right sides together. Press and then trim away the excess while basting. This can create a bit of waste (though I generally just add this extra fabric to stash), but it's fast and simple.

BASTE

To baste your finished quilt top, give your backing and top a really good press. Lay your backing, right side down, on the floor. (Use a hard floor. Carpet and rugs are a terrible mix with either glue or pins.) Use masking or packing tape to keep your backing taut and in place.

Lay your batting down flat over your backing. And then lay your quilt top, right side up, over your batting. If you're using basting pins, pin at this stage around 4" apart.

If you glue baste, try and rope in a helper! It'll go twice as fast and require half as much bending over. Open up the windows and/or doors to allow for good air flow. Lift one side of the batting and quilt top together and fold it over to the other side. Spray the exposed batting and backing according to the directions on the can. Lay the folded batting and quilt top back in place and spread out flat. Fold back the opposite side in the same manner and spray. Lay back out flat. Next lift one side of the quilt top only and fold it over the other half. Spray the exposed quilt top back and batting. Lay back in place and spread out flat. Repeat with the other side of the quilt top.

TRIM

Trim your backing and batting in line with the quilt top. If you have waited to trim your quilt top until now, trim all layers in line with ¼" from where the papers have been.

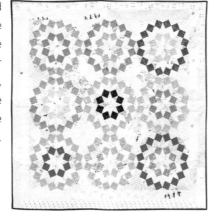

QUILTING

You can either machine or hand quilt your finished quilt tops. Machine quilting is faster, but hand quilting will make a beautiful quilt even more special. I tend to hand quilt because I prefer how quiet and relaxed it is compared to wrangling a quilt through my machine. I have noted in each pattern how I quilted that quilt.

To hand quilt, thread your needle and tie a knot at the other end of the thread. Put your needle into the quilt a little away from where you intend to stitch your design. Only punch your needle through the quilt top and batting layers. Bring your needle back up through the quilt top where you want your quilting line to start and pull the thread through. When the knot gets to the quilt top, carefully pull it through the fabric to hide the knot. It will catch in the batting and stay secured there. When you come to the end of your thread after stitching, tie another knot a ¼" or so from the quilt top. Put the needle back into the quilt, just going through the top layers again. Bring the needle back up and carefully pull the knot through to hide it.

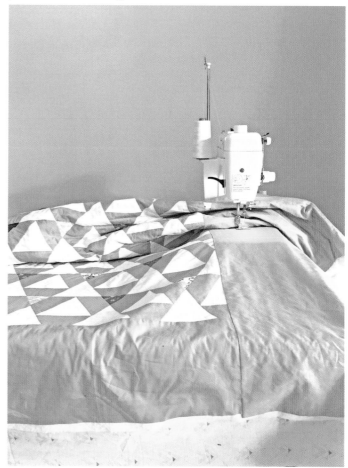

BINDING

Cut your binding fabric into 2 ½" x Width of Fabric (WOF) strips. Sew the binding strips together end to end using diagonal seams and then press the binding in half, wrong sides together. Sew the binding to the quilt top side. Leaving an 8" tail of binding, line up the raw edges of the quilt and the binding and sew ¼" from the edge through all layers.

When you get to a corner, stop sewing ¼" away from the edge of the quilt and back stitch. Fold the binding away from the quilt to make a diagonal fold coming from the corner, and so that the binding lines up with the next quilt edge. Use your finger to hold the fold in place and bring the binding back over the quilt so that the next fold lines up with the previous edge of the quilt. Sew the following edge from the fold.

Stop approximately 12" from where you started. Lay both loose ends of binding flat along quilt edge. Where these two loose ends meet, fold them back on themselves and press to form a crease. Using this crease as your stitching line, sew the two open ends of the binding together right sides together. Trim seam to ¼" and press open. Finish sewing binding to quilt.

To finish the binding, fold the binding over the to the back of the quilt. I mostly hand sew my bindings in place using the same stitch as above in the Applique section with 50 wt cotton thread. You can also use Perle cotton and stitch the binding down in a quilting style stitch, but only going through the binding and backing layers. Miter the corners as you move around the quilt.

If my quilt is a gift, and will receive lots of washes in its lifetime, or if I'm just in a hurry, I'll machine stitch my binding down. To machine stitch the binding, fold the binding under the quilt and place the quilt in the machine, quilt top side up. Stitch in the ditch between the binding and quilt top so that your stitches sew the binding in place underneath. Miter the corners as you move around the quilt and feed them carefully under the needle.

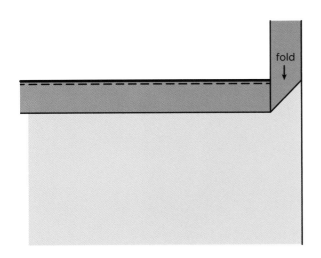

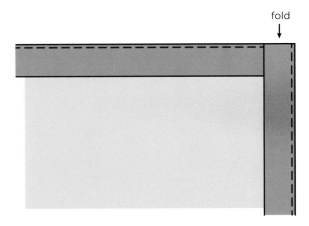

QUILTS

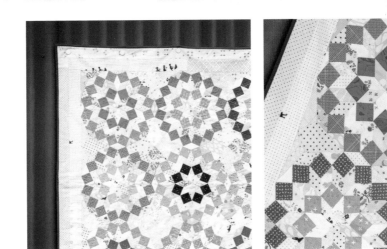

MYRTLE

The pretty, puffy, white flowers of the Myrtle tree inspired this quilt block. For the panel, I used different colours for each round, but for the quilt, I gathered all my low volume scraps for the diamonds to make the rings of squares stand out.

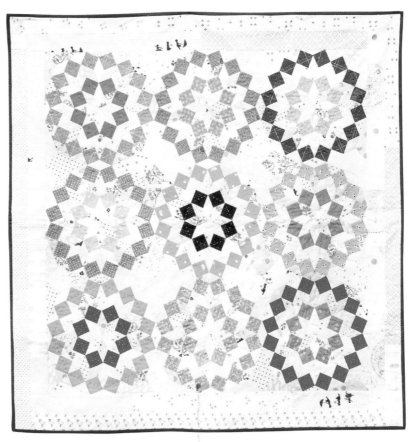

Finished Quilt Size - 45″ x 45″
Panel Size - 20½″ x 20½″

MYRTLE BLOCK

1 Take 8 diamonds and lay them out to form a star.

2 First, sew the diamonds into pairs. Then sew the pairs into half-stars and sew the halves into a star.

3 Stitch the middle squares around the outside of the star.

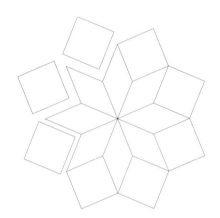

4 Take 2 of the diamonds, and starting at the wide angle, sew them together until you get to the point. Open the shapes out, take the third diamond, and stitch it to the pair, starting from the point to the wide angle. Make 8 diamond trios.

5 Sew the trios around middle squares.

6 Stitch along the seams between the trios.

7 Sew 16 squares around the outside of the block.

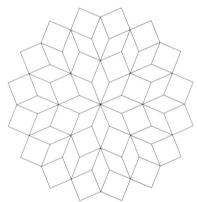

MYRTLE PANEL

PANEL SIZE 20 ½" x 20 ½"

SHAPE REQUIREMENTS
- (40) 2" 8-point Diamonds
- (24) 2" Squares
- (8) 2" Half Square Triangles
- (8) Edge Pieces

FABRIC REQUIREMENTS
- (32) Scraps at least 2 ¼" x 4 ¼" for the diamonds
- 2 ¾" x 22" strip for first round of squares
- 2 ¾" x WOF strip for second round of squares
- (2) 2 ¼" x WOF strips for outside round of diamonds and half square triangles
- ¼ yard for corner pieces
- 4" x WOF strip for border

CUTTING
Cut a ⅜" seam allowance around each paper template.

(Note: Edge pieces are directional! Cut 4 facing left and 4 facing right.)
Cut (2) 2" strips for the borders.

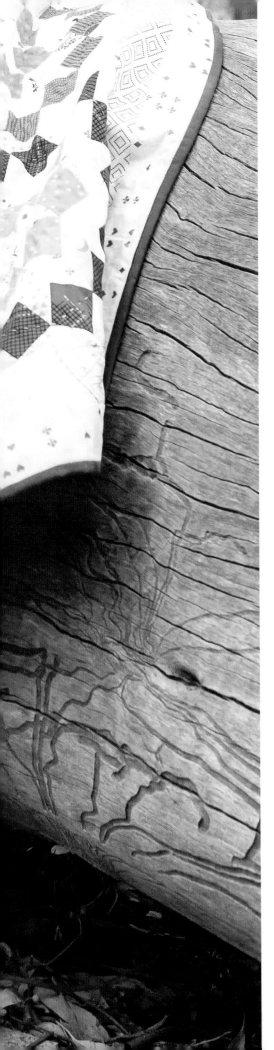

INSTRUCTIONS

1 Prepare all the shapes by basting the fabric to the paper templates.

2 Make 1 Myrtle Block.

3 Sew a half square triangle and diamond alternately around block.

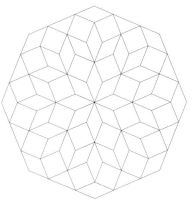

4 Sew the left and right edge pieces together in pairs. Sew edge blocks around the block.

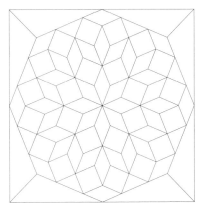

5 Remove papers and press. Trim the block ¼" from where the papers have been.

6 Sew a border strip to the top and bottom of the block. Press. Trim in line with the edges of the block.

7 Sew a border strip to the sides of the block. Press and trim.

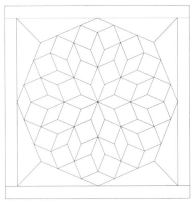

8 Trim the completed block to 20 ½" square.

MYRTLE QUILT

FINISHED QUILT SIZE 45" x 45"

SHAPE REQUIREMENTS

- (216) 1 ½" Squares
- (348) 1 ½" 8-point Diamonds
- (72) 1 ½" Half Square Triangles
- (24) 4-point Stars
- (24) Half Stars (edge pieces)

FABRIC REQUIREMENTS

- 2 ½" yards of low volume fabrics (shapes and border)
- 1 yard of bright coloured fabrics (18 F8ths)
- ⅓ yard for binding
- 2 yards for backing
- 53" x 53" batting

CUTTING

SQUARES

Cut a 2 ¼" strip x 18" for the middle squares (8 per strip) and a 2 ¼" strip x WOF for the outside squares (16 per strip).

DIAMONDS

Cut (21) 1 ¾" x WOF strips (or equivalent in scraps) and cut with a ⅜" seam allowance around the paper templates (17 per strip).

HALF SQUARE TRIANGLES

Cut (4) 1 ¾" x WOF strips and cut with a ⅜" seam allowance around the paper templates.
4-point Stars and Edge pieces: Cut a ⅜" seam allowance around the paper templates.

BORDER

(8) 2 ½" x WOF strips (or equivalent from scraps)

INSTRUCTIONS

1 Prepare all the shapes by basting the fabric to the paper templates.

2 Note that the edge shapes are directional! You'll need to baste 12 shapes pointing left and 12 pointing right.

3 Make 9 Myrtle blocks.

4 Lay out the quilt blocks in three rows of three to check for balanced colour placement. Number the blocks 1 – 9 starting from the top left-hand corner, 1-3 in the top row, 4-6 in the middle row, and 7-9 in the bottom row.

5 Starting with a half square triangle, sew a low volume half square triangle and diamond alternately around blocks 1-4 and 6-9, leaving a single space in the final gap for the overlapping diamond. (Mark this space with a clip to remember!)

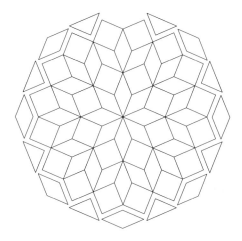

6 In block 5, leave a space (marked with a clip) for an overlapping diamond at the top, bottom, left and right of the block. Fill the remaining spaces with half square triangles and diamonds.

7 Sew two 4-point stars together along the short edge. Sew together a second pair.

8 Sew the pairs together to make a star. Make (4) stars.

9 Sew a left and right edge piece to the short sides of a 4-point star. Make (8) edge blocks.

10 Sew a left and right edge piece together along the short side. Make 4 corner blocks.

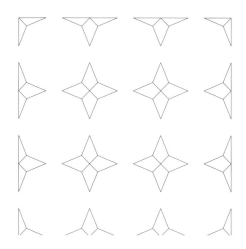

11 Sew the blocks together into 3 rows of 3, taking note in the diagram of the placement of the overlapping diamonds.

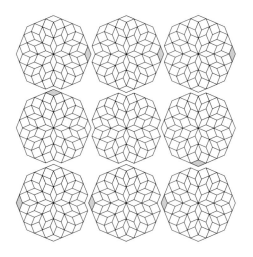

12 Sew the corner and edges blocks in the gaps above the first row.

13 Sew edge blocks and stars in the gaps below the first row. Sew the second row to the first row.

14 Sew edge blocks and stars in the gaps below the second row. Sew the third row to the second row.

15 Sew the corner and edges blocks in the gaps below the third row.

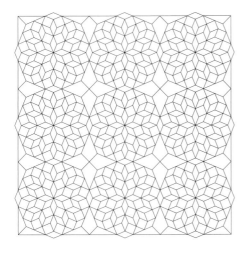

16 Take the papers out and press. Press the seams out at the top and bottom and sides of the quilt top.

17 Trim the quilt top a ¼" from where the papers have been.

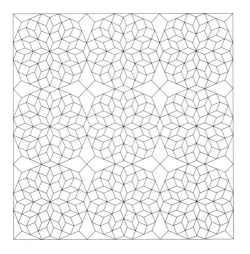

18 Sew the border strips together end to end to make a single long strip.

19 Line the end of the strip up with the edge of the quilt top and machine sew the border to the top. Trim the strip in line with the edge of the quilt top and press.

20 Line the end of the strip up with the next edge of the quilt top and machine sew the border to the side. Trim the strip in line with the edge of the quilt top and press.

21 Continue adding border strips around the quilt top until the quilt has two rounds of borders. Press.

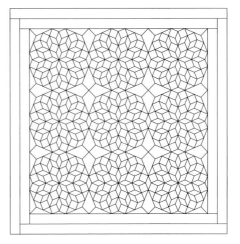

22 Layer the quilt back, right side down, batting and quilt top, right side up, and baste. Quilt as desired. I quilted thround the squares to make rings on each block.

23 Trim the backing and batting to match the edges of the quilt top. Bind the quilt.

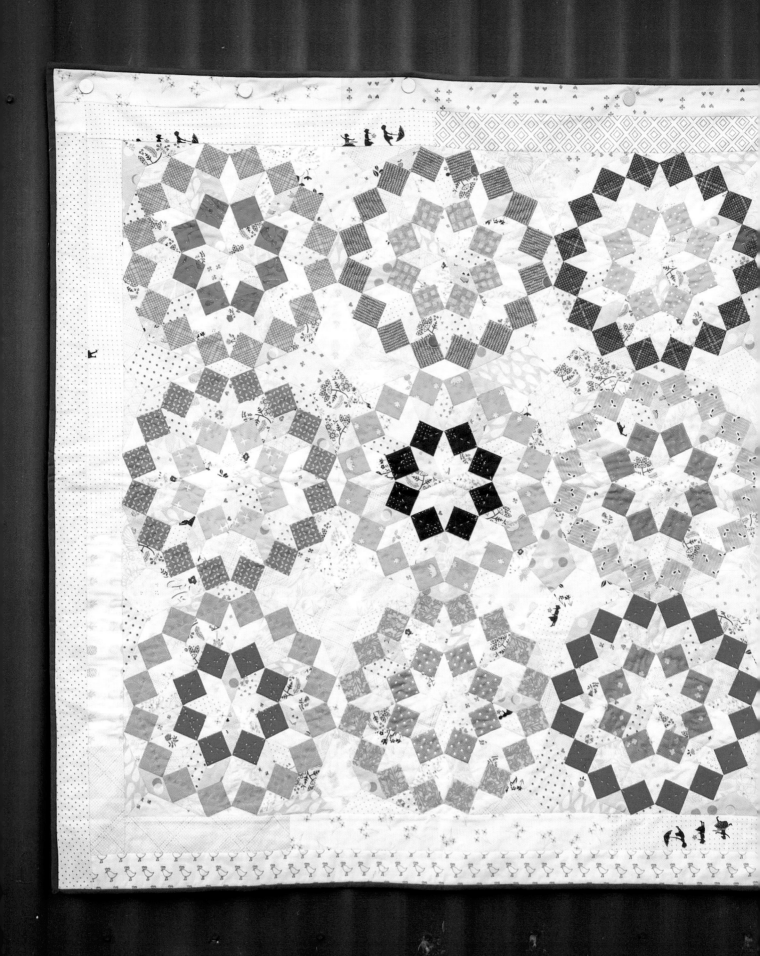

1½″ Quilt Templates

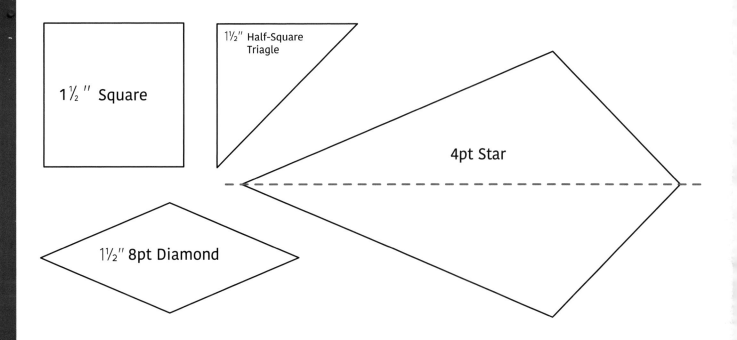

1½″ Square

1½″ Half-Square Triagle

4pt Star

1½″ 8pt Diamond

2″ Panel Templates

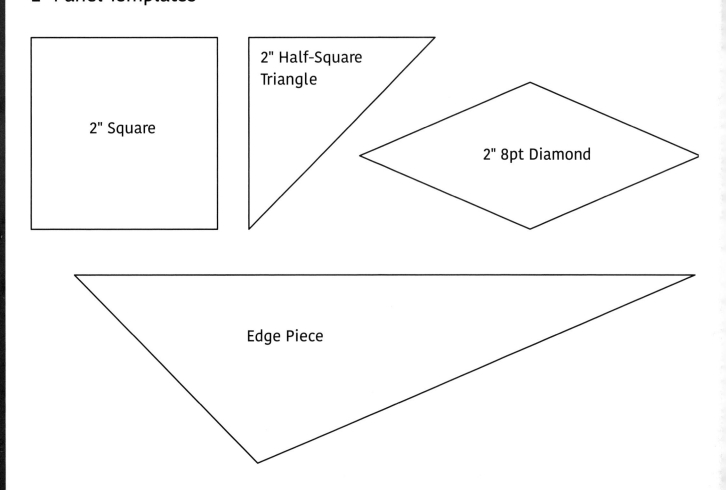

2″ Square

2″ Half-Square Triangle

2″ 8pt Diamond

Edge Piece

CARAWAY

Caraway is a great quilt for a beginner who wants to dip their toes in EPP and still end up with a large lap quilt. Choose your favourite collection of long-stashed treasures, and then those rectangles sew together fast! I used Crowns, or Third Hexagons, to create sweet little rows of plant shoots.

Finished Quilt Size - 45" x 45"
Panel Size - 20 ½" x 20 ½"

CARAWAY BLOCK

1 Take 2 matching, coloured crowns, place right sides together and stitch along one of the 1 ¾" length sides.

2 Sew a white crown into the crevice of the block, completing the hexagon.

CARAWAY PANEL

PANEL SIZE 7 ½" x 20 ½"

SHAPE REQUIREMENTS
- (30) 2" Crowns
- (6) 2" 6-pt Diamonds
- (12) 2" Equilateral Triangles

FABRIC REQUIREMENTS
- ¼ yard of coloured prints.
- ¼ yard of low volume/white.

CUTTING

(2) 2 ½" x 3 ½" rectangles in (10) different prints
(10) 2 ½" x 3 ½" rectangles in low volume/white (for the crowns)
(2) 2 ½" x WOF strips. Cut (6) diamonds and (12) triangles with a ⅜" seam allowance around the paper templates.

INSTRUCTIONS

1 Prepare all the pieces for the panel by basting the fabric to the paper templates.

2 Make 10 Caraway blocks.

3 Layout the blocks into 2 rows of 5 blocks. Stitch the blocks in row 1 to the blocks below them in row 2.

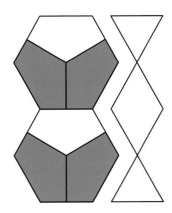

4 Sew an upside-down triangle to the top, right side of the first pair. Continue with a diamond in the crevice and a triangle below the diamond.

5 Repeat with remaining 4 block pairs.

6 Sew the pairs together into the quilt panel. Add a triangle, diamond, triangle to the left side of the panel.

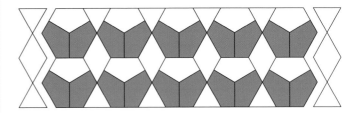

7 Take the papers out and press. Press the seams out at the top and bottom and sides of the rows.

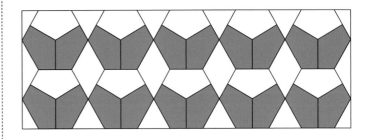

8 Trim all sides of the panel ¼" from where the papers have been.

CARAWAY QUILT

FINISHED SIZE 64" x 69"

SHAPE REQUIREMENTS
- (288) 2" Crowns
- (204) 2" Equilateral Triangles

FABRIC REQUIREMENTS
- 1 ¼ yds of white fabric
- At least 18 fat quarters of various prints
- ⅔ yd for binding
- 4 ½ yds for backing
- 72" x 77" batting

CUTTING

COLOURED CROWNS
(32) 2 ½" by half WOF strips and recut to 3 ½" x 2 ½" rectangles (6 per strip). (192 total)

WHITE CROWNS
(8) 2 ½" x WOF strips and recut to 3 ½" rectangles. (96 total)

TRIANGLES
(10) 2 ½" x WOF strips. Cut with a ⅜" seam allowance around the paper template. (22 per strip) (24) 8 ½" x 16 ½" rectangles in various prints

INSTRUCTIONS

1 Prepare all the pieces for the quilt by basting the fabric to the paper templates.

2 Make 96 blocks.

3 Sew a triangle to the top and bottom right hand sides of the hexagons.

4 Sew the blocks into pairs.

5 Sew the pairs together into rows of 4. The rows of four into 8, and then 8 into 16. You should have 6 rows of 16 in total.

6 Sew a triangle to the top and bottom left hand sides of each row.

7 Take the papers out and press. Press the seams out at the top and bottom and sides of the rows.

8 Trim the rows at the top, bottom and sides of each row, a ¼" from where the papers have been.

9 Lay out large rectangle pieces and crown rows according to the diagram - 4 rectangles in each row, with a crown row beneath each row of rectangles. Check for pleasing arrangement.

10 Sew the rectangles together along the short sides to make a row of 4. Make 6 rows.

11 Sew the top rectangle row to the crown row below. First place the crowns over the rectangles. Pin the rows together so that the points between every 4th hexagon sit directly below the seam between rectangles. Machine sew the rows together, with the crown row on top. This helps you keep all the seams going the right way as you put it through the machine. Press the seam towards the rectangles

12 Sew all the crown rows below the rectangle rows and press.

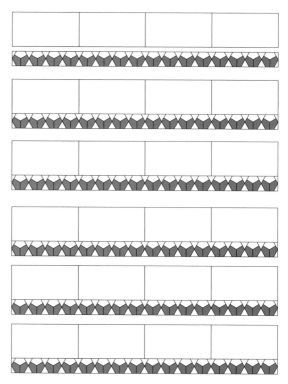

13 Sew the rows together to complete the quilt top.

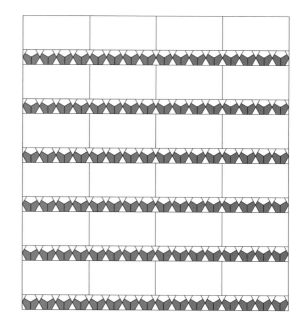

14 Layer the quilt back, right side down, batting and quilt top, right side up, and baste. Quilt as desired. I hand quilted in dense, horizontal lines through the large rectangle sections.

15 Trim the backing and batting to match the edges of the quilt top. Bind the quilt.

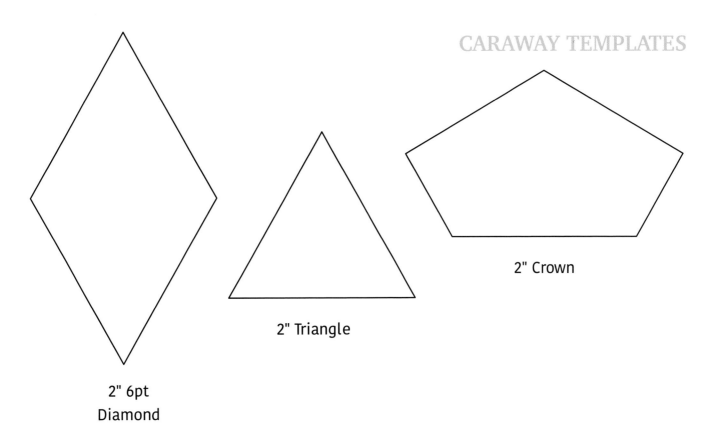

2" 6pt
Diamond

2" Triangle

2" Crown

PEPPERMINT

So many fabric designs are a work of art in themselves.
I designed this quilt to feature one of my favourite prints, and
chose the leaf-colour fabrics to match. These spunky little
stems of leaves remind me of the voracious growth and spicy
taste of one of my favourite plants.

Panel Size - 10 ⅛" x 29 ¼"
Finished Quilt Size: 26" x 41"

PEPPERMINT BLOCK

1 Prepare all the pieces by basting the fabric to the paper templates.

2 Take 2 diamonds, and sew from the wider angle to the point, and without cutting your thread, sew a third diamond to these.

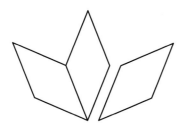

3 Sew a square above each join.

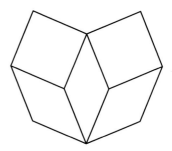

PEPPERMINT PANEL

PANEL SIZE 10 ⅛" x 29 ¼"

SHAPE REQUIREMENTS

◆ (48) 2" Diamonds
◆ (32) 2" Squares
◆ (15) Edge Triangle A (half Diamond)
◆ (2) Edge Triangle B (quarter Diamond)
◆ (1) Edge Triangle C (isosceles Triangle)

FABRIC REQUIREMENTS

◆ (16) scraps at least 2 ¼" x 10" for the Diamonds
◆ (1) scrap at least 2 ¼" x 2 ½" for Edge Triangle C
◆ ¼ yd background fabric

CUTTING

DIAMONDS

Cut a ⅜" seam allowance around the paper templates.

EDGE TRIANGLE C

Cut a ⅜" seam allowance around Edge Triangle C.

SQUARES

(3) 2 ¾" x WOF strips of background fabric.
Recut to (32) 2 ¾" squares.

EDGE TRIANGLES A AND B

Cut a ⅜" around (15) Edge triangle A and (2) Edge Triangle B with remaining background fabric. (Note: Triangle B is directional! Cut and baste 1 facing left and 1 facing right.)

INSTRUCTIONS

1 Prepare all the pieces by basting the fabric to the paper templates.

2 Make (15) Peppermint blocks

3 Make (1) extra leaf trio without sewing the squares above.

4 Sew a square to the left-hand side of an edge triangle C. Continue stitching down the right side with a second square.

5 Layout your blocks in 2 columns. Place 7 blocks, with a leaf trio at the top, and an edge block at the bottom in the first column and 8 complete blocks in the second column.

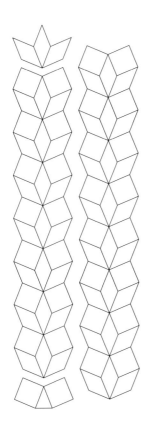

6 Sew the first block in column 1 to the block below it. Continue adding blocks until the column is complete. Sew all the blocks into 2 columns.

7 Sew a Triangle A into the top left crevice of the first column. Continue stitching (8) Edge Triangle A into the crevices between the blocks.

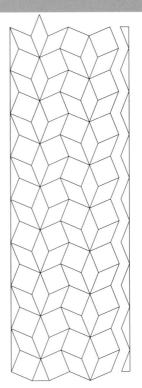

8 Sew column 2 to column 1.

9 Sew a Triangle B into the top right corner of the final column. Continue stitching (7) Edge Triangle A into the crevices between the blocks. Complete the edge with another Triangle B.

10 Take the papers out and press. Press the seams out at the top and bottom and sides of the rows.

Trim the panel at the top, bottom and sides, a ¼" from where the papers have been.

PEPPERMINT QUILT

FINISHED QUILT SIZE 26" x 41"

SHAPE REQUIREMENTS

🍃 (90) 2" Squares

🍃 (135) 2" 8-point Diamonds

🍃 (8) Edge Triangle A (Half Diamond)

🍃 (4) Edge Triangle B (Quarter Diamond)

🍃 (4) Edge Triangle C (Isosceles Triangle)

FABRIC REQUIREMENTS

🍃 1 yd fabric in various prints for Peppermint leaves

🍃 ½ yd for background fabric

🍃 ¼ yd feature print

🍃 ⅓ yd for binding

🍃 2 yds for backing

🍃 34" x 49" batting

CUTTING

DIAMONDS

(12) 2 ¼" x WOF strips in various prints, then cut ⅜" seam allowance around the diamonds in groups of 3. (4 leaf trios per strip).

EDGE TRIANGLE C

Cut a ⅜" seam allowance around (4) Edge Triangle C with remaining print fabric.

SQUARES

(6) 2 ¾" x WOF strips, recut into (90) 2 ¾" squares.

EDGE TRIANGLES A AND B

Cut a ⅜" seam allowance around (8) Edge triangle A and (4) Edge Triangle B with remaining background fabric. (Note: Triangle B is directional! Cut and baste 2 facing left and 2 facing right.)

(1) 8 ½" x WOF rectangle of feature print.

INSTRUCTIONS

1 Prepare all the pieces by basting the fabric to the paper templates.

2 Make (41) Peppermint blocks

3 Make (4) extra leaf trios without sewing the squares above.

4 Sew a square to the left-hand side of an edge triangle C. Continue stitching down the right side with a second square. Make 4 edge blocks.

5 Layout your blocks in 9 columns. Place 5 complete blocks in the odd columns and 4 blocks, with a leaf trio at the top, and an edge block at the bottom in the even columns.

6 Check for pleasing colour placement and number columns.

7 Sew the first block in column 1 to the block below it. Continue adding blocks until the column is complete. Sew all the blocks into columns.

8 Sew column 2 to column 1. Then attach column 3, and so on until all the columns are sewn together.

9 Sew a Triangle B into the top left corner of the first column. Continue stitching (4) Edge Triangle A's into the crevices between the blocks. Complete the edge with another Triangle B.

10 Sew a Triangle B into the top right corner of the final column. Continue stitching (4) Edge Triangle A's into the crevices between the blocks. Complete the edge with another Triangle B.

11 Take the papers out and press. Press the seams out at the top and bottom and sides of the rows.

12 Trim the quilt top at the top, bottom and sides, a ¼" from where the papers have been.

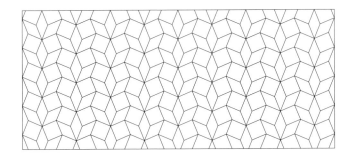

13 Centre the feature print strip over the bottom of the quilt top and pin to stop the top moving. Machine sew together. Press.

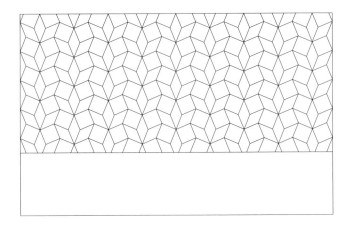

14 Layer the quilt back, right side down, batting and quilt top, right side up, and baste. Quilt as desired. I hand quilted Peppermint with vertical lines through the leaves and horizontal lines through the feature print.

15 Trim the backing and batting to match the edges of the quilt top. Bind the quilt.

PEPPERMINT TEMPLATES

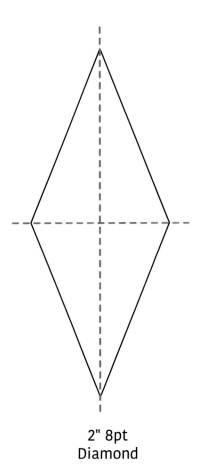

2" 8pt Diamond

2" Square

YARROW

Yarrow flowers have a tiny, busy centre, with little, flat petals around it, just like this vintage hexie star block. The simple, two-colour blocks are perfect for scrap busting or fussy cutting – or a little bit of both!

Panel Size – 8 ½″ x 35″
Finished Quilt Size: 54″ x 54″

YARROW BLOCK

1 Take 6 diamonds and lay them out to form a star.

2 Take 2 of the diamonds, and starting at the wide angle, sew them together until you get to the point. Open the shapes out, take the third diamond, and stitch it to the pair to make a half star. Stitch the second half together.

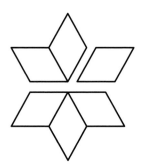

3 Sew hexagons into the crevices of the star.

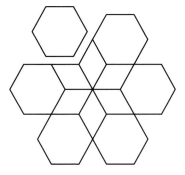

4 Sew diamonds into the gaps between the hexagons.

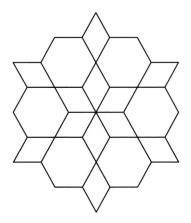

YARROW PANEL

PANEL SIZE 8 ½" x 35"

SHAPE REQUIREMENTS
- (80) 1" 6-point Diamonds
- (30) 1" Hexagons
- (20) 1" Edge Shapes
- (8) 2" Edge Shapes
- (4) Corner Pieces

FABRIC REQUIREMENTS
- (5) 1 ½" x 22" strips in various prints for the diamonds
- (5) 2 ½" x 18" strips in various prints for the hexagons
- 13" x WOF strip for background fabric

CUTTING

YARROW BLOCKS

DIAMONDS

Cut a ⅜" seam allowance around the template from the 1 ½" strips. 12 per strip.

HEXAGONS

Cut a ⅜" seam allowance around the template from the 2 ½" strips. 6 per strip.

JOINING BLOCKS

DIAMONDS

(1) 1 ½" WOF strip. Cut a ⅜" seam allowance around the template. Cut 20.

1" EDGE SHAPES

(2) 2 ¼" strips. Set the template on the strip pointing up like a house. Cut a ⅜" seam allowance around the template. Cut 20.

2" EDGE SHAPES

(1) 3 ¾" x WOF strip. Set the template on the strip pointing up like a house. Cut a ⅜" seam allowance around the template. Cut 8.

CORNER PIECES

Cut a ⅜" seam allowance around the template. Cut 4. (Note: Corner pieces are directional! Cut 2 facing left and 2 facing right.)

INSTRUCTIONS

1 Prepare all the shapes by basting the fabric to the paper templates.

2 Make 5 Yarrow Blocks.

3 Place 2 joining diamonds right sides together and stitch along one side to make an arrow. Make 8 arrows.

4 Set the 2" edge shape pointing up like a house. Sew the diamond arrow above the point. Sew the remaining diamond arrows to the 2" edge shapes.

5 Set the 1" edge shape pointing up like a house. Sew (2) 1" edge shapes beside each other. Make 10 pairs of 1" edge shapes.

6 Sew a diamond to the right side of the right facing corner piece so that bottom edges of both shapes line up. Repeat with second right facing corner piece. Sew diamonds to the left side of the left facing corner pieces.

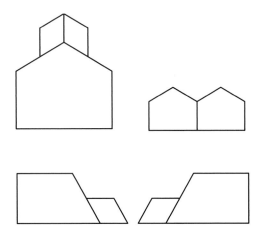

7 Lay out your blocks in a column and number them 1-5.

8 Sew the pairs of 1" edge shapes into the crevices on each side of each block.

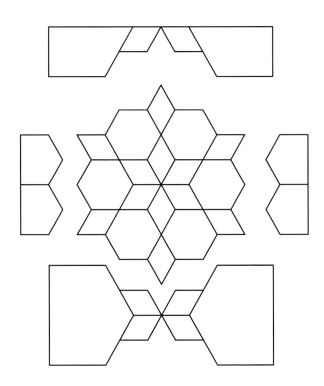

9 Place the right facing corner piece above the left side of the first block. Sew it in place.

10 Continue stitching around the top right of the block with the left facing corner piece.

11 Sew a 2" edge unit under each side of the first block.

12 Sew the second block below the first.

13 Continue stitching edge units and then Yarrow blocks until the 5th block.

14 Sew corner pieces below the 5th block.

15 Remove papers and press. Press the seams out at the top and bottom and sides of the panel. Trim the panel ¼" from where the papers have been.

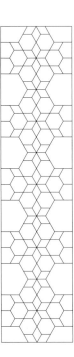

56

YARROW QUILT

FINISHED QUILT SIZE 54" x 54"

SHAPE REQUIREMENTS

- (1022) 1" 6-point Diamonds
- (336) 1" Hexagons
- (42) 2" Hexagons
- (14) 2" Half Hexagons
- (12) 2" Vertical Half Hexagons
- (4) Corner Pieces

FABRIC REQUIREMENTS

- 1 ¾ yards of background fabric
- (56) 2 ½" x 18" strips in various prints
- (56) 1 ½" x 22" strips in various prints
- ½ yard for binding
- 3 ½ yards for backing
- 62" x 62" batting

CUTTING

YARROW BLOCKS

DIAMONDS

Cut a ⅜" seam allowance around the template from the 1 ½" strips. 12 per strip.

HEXAGONS

Cut a ⅜" seam allowance around the template from the 2 ½" strips. 6 per strip

JOINING BLOCKS

DIAMONDS

(6) 1 ½" WOF strips. Cut a ⅜" seam allowance around the template. Cut 126.

2" HEXAGONS

(5) 4 ¼" x WOF strips. Centre the template on the strip with the flat edge at the top. Cut a ⅜" seam allowance around the template. Cut 42.

VERTICAL HALF HEXAGONS

(2) 2 ½" x WOF strips. Set the template on the strip pointing up like a house. Cut a ⅜" seam allowance around the template. Cut 12. Use the remaining fabric for the half hexagons.

HALF HEXAGONS

(1) 2 ½" x WOF strip. Set the template on the strip with the centre, short edge at the top. Cut a ⅜" seam allowance around the template. Flip the paper template and fit it ⅜" from the previous cut. Cut a ⅜" seam allowance around the template. Cut 14.

CORNER PIECES

Cut a ⅜" seam allowance around the template. Cut 4. (Note: Corner pieces are directional! Cut and baste 2 facing left and 2 facing right.)

BORDERS (6) 3 ½" x WOF. Cut (2) of the strips in half to make (4) 3 ½" x 22" strips.

INSTRUCTIONS

1 Prepare all the shapes by basting the fabric to the paper templates.

2 Make 56 Yarrow blocks.

3 Lay out the quilt blocks in 7 rows of 8 to check for balanced colour placement. Take a photo on your phone for reference.

4 Sew 2 background diamonds into the crevices on the right side of every block.

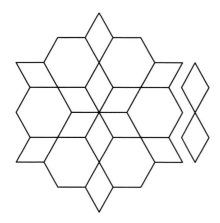

5 Sew 2 background diamonds into the crevices on the left side of the first block in each row.

6 Sew block 1 from the first row to block 2. Add block 3, and then 4 and so on, until you have 8 blocks in a row. Make 7 rows.

7 Place 2 joining diamonds right sides together and stitch along one side to make an arrow. Make 96 arrows.

8 Set the 2" hexagon with the flat side at the top. Sew the arrows to the left and right points of each 2" hexagon.

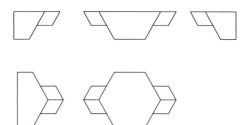

9 Sew an arrow to the centre point of each vertical half hexagon.

10 Set a half hexagon so that the centre, short side is at the top. Sew a single diamond to the bottom left and right of each half hexagon so that bottom edges of all shapes line up.

11 Sew a diamond to the right side of the right facing corner piece so that bottom edges of both shapes line up. Repeat with second right facing corner piece. Sew diamonds to the left side of the left facing corner pieces.

12 Sew the corner and half hexagon edge blocks in the gaps above the first row.

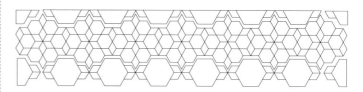

13 Sew vertical half hexagon edge blocks and joining blocks in the gaps below rows 1-6.

14 Sew the corner and half hexagon edge blocks in the gaps below the 7th row.

15 Sew row 1 to row 2. Then row 3 to 4, and 5 to 6.

16 Sew 1-2 to 3-4 and 5-6 to 7. Sew the two halves of the quilt together.

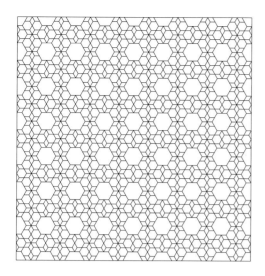

17 Take the papers out and press. Press the seams out at the top and bottom and sides of the quilt top.

18 Trim the quilt top a ¼" from where the papers have been.

19 Sew together one each of the WOF border strips with a 22" strip. Press. Make 4.

20 Line the end of the strip up with the edge of the quilt top and machine sew the border to the top. Trim the strip in line with the edge of the quilt top and press.

21 Line the end of the strip up with the opposite of the quilt top and machine sew the border to the side. Trim the strip in line with the edge of the quilt top and press.

22 Add a border strip to the top and bottom of the quilt. Trim any excess.

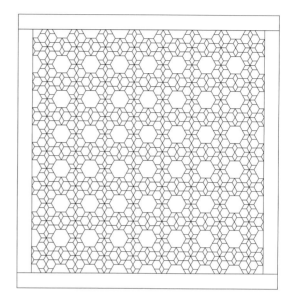

23 Layer the quilt back, right side down, batting and quilt top, right side up, and baste. Quilt as desired. I hand quilted Yarrow with diagonal lines through the stars and diamonds.

24 Trim the backing and batting to match the edges of the quilt top. Bind the quilt.

YARROW TEMPLATES

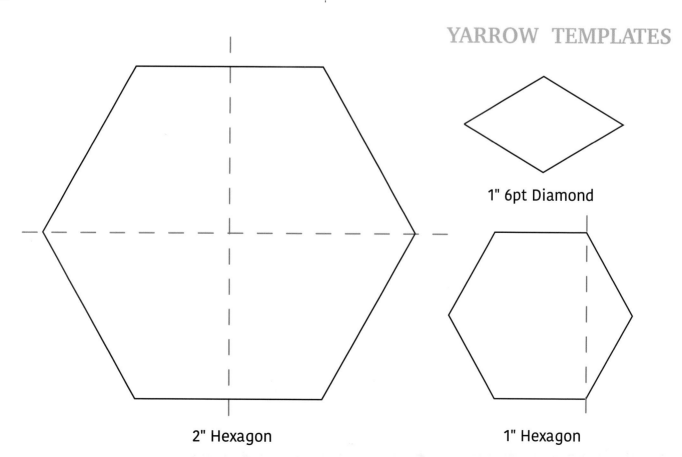

1" 6pt Diamond

2" Hexagon

1" Hexagon

HONEYSUCKLE

These happy, growing honeycomb vines evoke feelings of sweetness and joy for me, just like the plant! There are so many fun ways to use this vine, that I made three different versions! The first uses 1" honeycombs, perfect for little scraps or mini charm squares. The second is a large vine stitched to a pieced panel so that the colours can come in and out of focus from the background, just like flowers in a garden. The quilt is a simple collection of vines stitched to a whole cloth quilt.

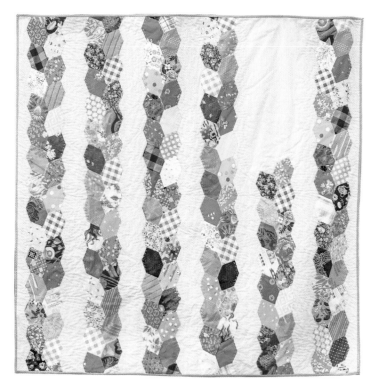

Panel A Size - 8 ½" x 42"
Panel B Size - 10 ½" x 65 ½"
Finished Quilt Size: 52" x 52"

HONEYSUCKLEBLOCK

The Honeysuckle Vine is a braid pattern that can be made as long or short as you need, and with any sized honeycombs.

1 Take 2 honeycombs and point the long axis of the left honeycomb slightly left. Point the long axis of the right honeycomb slightly right.

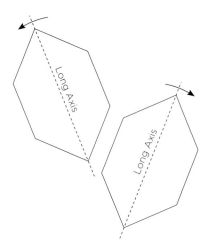

2 Sew the bottom, right edge of the left honeycomb to the left side edge of the right honeycomb.

3 Take another honeycomb and place the bottom, 90-degree angle of the honeycomb into the 90-degree angle created above the first two shapes. Sew along both sides.

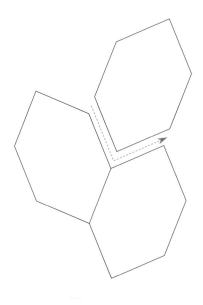

4 Keep adding honeycombs in the 90-degree crevice at the top of the vine until the row is complete.

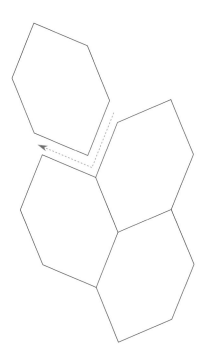

64

HONEYSUCKLE PANELS

PANEL A

PANEL SIZE 8 ½" x 42"

Note: Panel A includes Feverfew Blocks also. These are attached after the Seedlings quilt top is complete.

SHAPE REQUIREMENTS
🍂 (34) 1" Honeycombs

FABRIC REQUIREMENTS
🍂 (34) Scraps at least 2 ¼" x 3"
🍂 8 ½" x WOF strip for background

CUTTING
🍂 Cut a ⅜" seam allowance around each paper template.
🍂 Trim the selvedges from the background strip to make 8 ½" x 42".

PANEL B

PANEL SIZE 10 ½" x 65 ½"

SHAPE REQUIREMENTS
🍂 (35) 2" Honeycombs

FABRIC REQUIREMENTS
🍂 (35) Scraps at least 3 ½" x 5 ½"
🍂 (5) fat quarters of low volume or background fabric

CUTTING
🍂 Cut a ⅜" seam allowance around each paper template.
🍂 (5) 10 ½" x 13 ½" rectangles.

INSTRUCTIONS

1 Prepare all the shapes by basting the fabric to the paper templates.

2 Sew 34 honeycombs together into a Honeysuckle vine.

3 Take the papers out and press, making sure all the seams are tucked under the shapes.

4 Place the vine horizontally on the background strip 2" from the bottom of the strip and hanging over the right side of the strip so that the end of the seam will be covered when the top is sewn together.

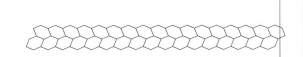

5 Machine or hand applique in place.

INSTRUCTIONS

1 Prepare all the shapes by basting the fabric to the paper templates.

2 Sew 35 honeycombs together into a Honeysuckle braid.

3 Take the papers out and press, making sure all the seams are tucked under the shapes.

4 Sew the rectangles together end to end along the short sides to make a long background strip.

5 Centre the vine horizontally on the background strip so that is runs from left to right.

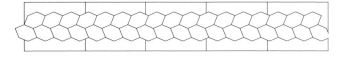

6 Hand or machine applique in place.

HONEYSUCKLE QUILT

FINISHED QUILT SIZE 52" x 52"

SHAPE REQUIREMENTS

🐚 (167) 2" Honeycombs

FABRIC REQUIREMENTS

🐚 (167) scraps of fabric at least 3 ½" x 5 ½"

🐚 3 ¼ yards of background fabric

🐚 ½ yard for binding

🐚 3 ½ yards for backing

🐚 60" x 60" batting

CUTTING

🐚 (2) 54" x WOF rectangles. Recut one of the pieces to 13" x 54".

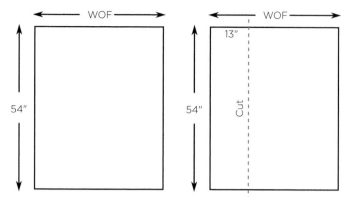

🐚 Trim scraps to ⅜" seam allowance around the honeycombs.

INSTRUCTIONS

1 Prepare all the shapes by basting the fabric to the paper templates.

2 Make (4) Honeysuckle vines of (30) honeycombs.

3 Make (1) Honeysuckle vine of (17) honeycombs.

4 Take the papers out and press, making sure all the seams are tucked under the shapes.

5 Place the large background rectangle and the small background rectangle right sides together aligned along the selvedge. Sew together. Press.

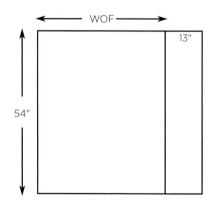

6 Layer the quilt back, right side down, batting and background fabric, right side up.

7 Lay the Honeysuckle vines in vertical columns over the quilt sandwich, parallel with the background fabric seam. Place a 3 ½" gap between each vine. Use basting pins to pin through the vines and the quilt sandwich.

8 Applique the vines to the quilt sandwich by quilting through all the layers, an ⅛" inside the edge of the vine.

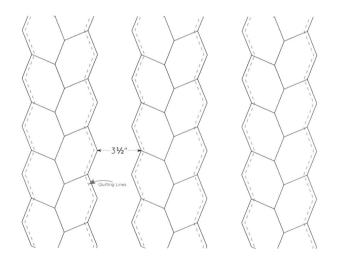

9 Add extra quilting as desired.

10 Trim the backing, batting and quilt top 1 ½" from the sides of each vine, and ¼" from where the papers have been at the top and bottom. Bind the quilt.

HONEYSUCKLE TEMPLATES

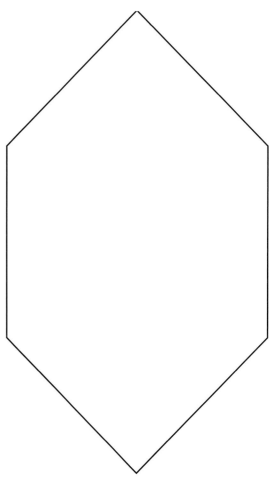

2" Honeycomb

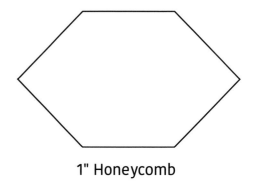

1" Honeycomb

FEVERFEW

Feverfew flowers have a wonderfully large centre, surrounded by cute little petals, just like these honeycomb blocks. I had a little play with fussy cutting for the mini quilt and collected scraps into colour groups for the panel so that you could see just how different a design can be, depending on how you colour it in!

Panel Size - 9″ x 43″
Finished Quilt Size: 28″ x 28″

FEVERFEW BLOCK

1 Place the honeycombs around the centre octagon so that they point slightly right and move around the octagon in a clockwise direction.

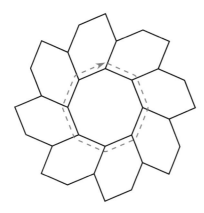

2 Place the first honeycomb over the octagon, right sides together and stitch along the seam.

3 Open the pieces out and place the next honeycomb over the octagon. Stitch.

4 Continue sewing the honeycombs around the octagon.

5 Stitch the seams between the honeycombs from the entre out.

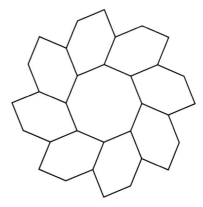

FEVERFEW PANEL

PANEL SIZE 9" x 43"

SHAPE REQUIREMENTS

🔖 (9) 1" Octagons
🔖 (72) 1" Honeycombs

FABRIC REQUIREMENTS

🔖 (9) Scraps at least 3" square
🔖 (72) Scraps at least 2 ¼" x 3" for the honeycombs, in colour groups of 8
🔖 9" x WOF strip for background fabric (check that the fabric is 43" wide inside the selvedges)

CUTTING

🔖 Cut a ⅜" seam allowance around each paper template.
🔖 Trim the selvedges from the background fabric to make the panel 43" wide.

INSTRUCTIONS

1 Prepare all the shapes by basting the fabric to the paper templates.

2 Make 9 Feverfew Blocks.

3 Lay out your blocks to make a row of 4, a row of 3 and a row of 2.

4 Stitch the blocks into these rows.

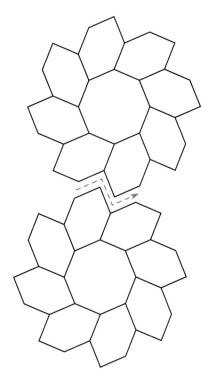

5 Take the papers out and press, making sure all the seams are tucked under the shapes.

6 Centre the first row of 4 flowers vertically on the panel, ½" from the top. Pin or glue in place. Centre the second row of 3 flowers vertically on the panel, ½" from the bottom. Pin or glue. (Panel 2) Leave the remaining pair of flowers for once the Seedlings quilt is sewn together.

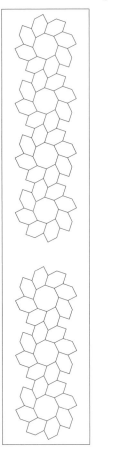

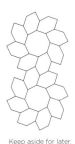

Keep aside for later.

7 Applique the flower rows to the panel.

FEVERFEW QUILT

I made the Feverfew mini quilt with fussy cut honeycombs. They are stitched together with little plusses between, and then appliqued to a background. Use small prints to get 8 repeats easily if fussy cutting.

FINISHED QUILT SIZE 28" x 28"

SHAPE REQUIREMENTS
- (16) 1" Octagons
- (128) 1" Honeycombs
- (36) 1" Houses

FABRIC REQUIREMENTS
- (16) Pieces at least 3" square
- (16) Fat quarters – half yards if fussy cutting.
- 1 yard background fabric
- ¼ yard for binding
- 1 yard for backing
- 36" x 36" batting

CUTTING

OCTAGONS
Cut a ⅜" seam allowance around each paper template.

HONEYCOMBS
Cut a ⅜" seam allowance around (8) honeycombs per (16) prints.

BACKGROUND
Cut (2) 2 ⅛" x WOF strips. Recut into (36) 1 ¾" x 2 ⅛" rectangles for houses.
Cut a 28" square for the background.

INSTRUCTIONS

1 Prepare all the shapes by basting the fabric to the paper templates.

2 Make (16) Feverfew Blocks.

3 Place 4 houses with the shortest sides pointing inwards to make a plus.

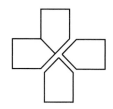

4 Sew the top and left houses together along the shortest edge. Sew the bottom and right houses together.

5 Place the two halves right sides together, matching up the centre seams. Stitch the 2 halves together.

6 Place blocks in 4 rows of 4 so that the petals in the sides and top and bottom are interlocking, with a plus in the gaps.

7 Sew the first block in row 1 to the second. Then add block 3 and 4.

8 Sew (3) plusses in the gaps below the joins between the blocks.

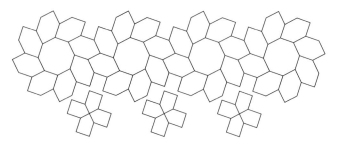

9 Sew the remaining blocks into rows. Stitch plusses under rows 2 and 3.

10 Sew row 1 to row 2. Then add 3 and 4.

11 Take the papers out and press, making sure all the seams are tucked under the shapes.

12 Centre the patchwork on the background square and pin or glue in place.

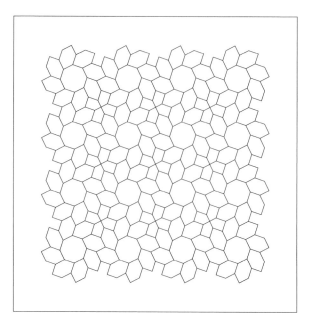

13 Applique the patchwork to the background.

14 Layer the quilt back, right side down, batting and quilt top, right side up, and baste. Quilt as desired. I hand quilted around each octagon and then followed around the edge of the applique.

15 Trim the backing and batting to match the edges of the quilt top. Bind the quilt.

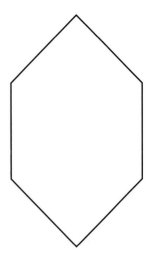

1" Honeycomb

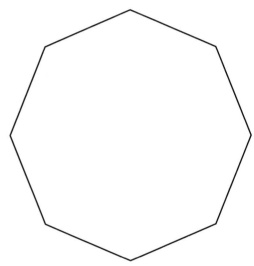

1" Octagon

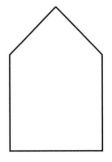

1" House

ELDERBERRY

The layout of these blocks for the Elderberry quilt was inspired by an old fan-like fabric by Anna Maria Horner, that I was fussy cutting for Feverfew! I had the little pentagons all basted and waiting for the right inspiration and was so excited when I found it!

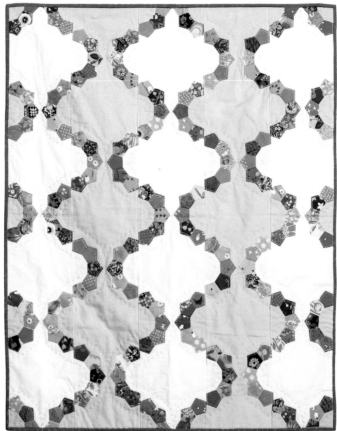

Panel Size - 7 ½" x 51 ¾"
Finished Quilt Size: 33" x 40"

ELDERBERRY BLOCK

1 Arrange 5 pentagons around the short sides of a half decagon. Stitch the pentagons to the half decagon.

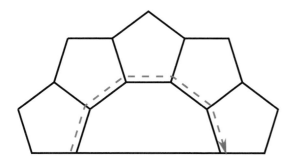

2 Stitch the seams between the pentagons.

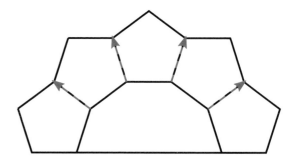

ELDERBERRY PANEL

PANEL SIZE 7 ½" x 51 ¾"

SHAPE REQUIREMENTS
- (45) 1" Pentagons
- (9) 1" Half Decagons

FABRIC REQUIREMENTS
- (45) scraps at least 2 ¼" square
- (9) scraps at least 2 ¼" x 4"
- ½ yd background fabric

CUTTING

Pentagons and Half Decagons: Cut a ⅜" seam allowance around the paper templates.

BACKGROUND FABRIC
- Cut (2) 7 ½" x WOF strips

INSTRUCTIONS

1 Prepare all the pieces by basting the fabric to the paper templates.

2 Make (9) Elderberry blocks

3 Take the papers out and press. Press the seams at the base of the block out but keep the seams around the semi-circle tucked under. Trim the base to ¼" from where the papers have been.

4 Sew the background strips together end to end. Press and trim to 52" long.

5 Fold the background strip in half, end to end, to find the centre.

6 Centre an Elderberry block at the top of the strip, facing down, using the fold as your guide. Line up the edge of the block base with the edge of the background. Glue to hold in place.

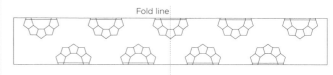

Fold line

7 Lay the remaining blocks out, alternating between the top and bottom, so that there are 5 blocks at the top of the panel, and 4 underneath. The blocks are 5 ½" apart at the base. Glue in place.

8 Applique by hand or top stitch around the points of the pentagons on each block.

9 Panel can be left slightly longer than needed until sewn to Seedlings quilt and trimmed.

ELDERBERRY QUILT

FINISHED QUILT SIZE 33" x 40"

SHAPE REQUIREMENTS

◈ (206) 1" Pentagons
◈ (34) 1" Half Decagon
◈ (12) 1" Quarter Decagon

FABRIC REQUIREMENTS

◈ (206) scraps at least 2 ¼" square
◈ ¾ yard of white fabric
◈ ⅔ yard of grey fabric
◈ ⅓ yd for binding
◈ 1 ⅓ yds for backing
◈ 41" x 48" batting

CUTTING

PENTAGONS

Cut a ⅜" seam allowance around the paper templates.

WHITE FABRIC

BACKGROUND

Cut (3) 7" x WOF.

HALF DECAGONS

Cut (2) 2 ¼" x WOF. Recut into (16) 4" x 2 ¼" rectangles.

GREY FABRIC

BACKGROUND

Cut (2) 7" x WOF.

HALF AND QUARTER DECAGONS

Cut (3) 2 ¼" x WOF. Recut into (18) 4" x 2 ¼" rectangles for the Half Decagons and (12) 2 ¼" squares for the Quarter Decagons.

INSTRUCTIONS

1 Prepare all the pieces by basting the fabric to the paper templates. Note: The quarter decagons are directional! Baste 6 with the shortest side on the left, and 6 with the shortest side on the right.

2 Make (16) Elderberry blocks with a white half decagon and (18) Elderberry blocks with a grey half decagon.

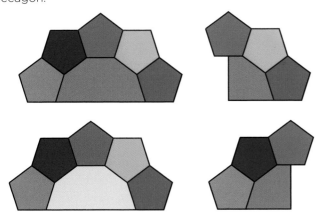

3 In the same fashion, sew (3) pentagons around the short sides of a grey quarter decagon to make a half block. Make (12) half blocks. (6) will have the final pentagon overhanging on the right and (6) on the left.

4 Take the papers out and press. Press all the seams under the block ready for applique.

The seams of the blocks that border the edges need to have those seam allowances pressed out so they can be sewn into the binding.

5 Lay out the 7" strips in this order: white, grey, white, grey, white. Machine sew them together. Press.

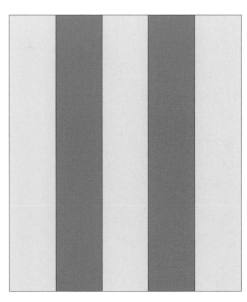

6 Fold your background panel in half, horizontally, and press to mark the centre line across the strips.

7 Along the centre fold line, place (6) grey blocks on the white strips in pairs, facing each other. Line up the base of the blocks with the seam between strips so that no white shows beside the block. Line up the point of the centre pentagon with the fold line.

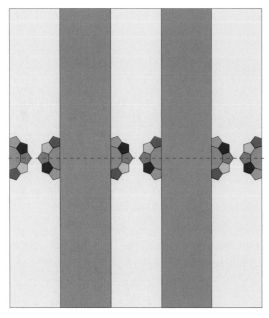

8 Use a little glue to hold in place.

9 Above and below the grey blocks, place white blocks on the grey strips. Rather than meeting the block points together, slide them until they overlap ¼". Glue in place.

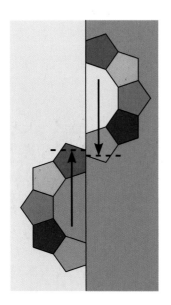

10 Continue adding blocks above and below until there are (16) white blocks on the grey panels and (18) grey blocks on the white panels. Add half blocks to the top so that the overhanging pentagons are at the top of the quilt. Do the same at the bottom.

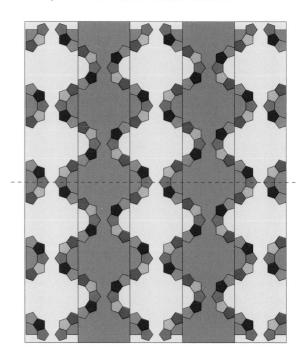

11 Using a sewing machine, top stitch in straight lines ⅛" each side of the seams between strips to applique the side edges of the block in place.

12 Starting at the top, left corner, top stitch around the points of the pentagons on each block down the left side of the quilt.

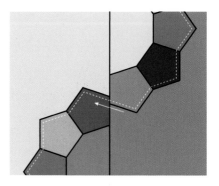

13 Start at the top again, in the next column of blocks. Top stitch around the points of the corner block, then continue stitching without breaking, down the curve of blocks on either side of the seam. Top stitch the points of the pentagons of all the blocks down this way.

14 Trim the quilt top on the sides, a ¼" from where the papers have been. Trim at the top and bottom a ¼" from the base of the quarter decagons.

15 Layer the quilt back, right side down, batting and quilt top, right side up, and baste. Quilt as desired. For this quilt, I shadowed the curves created by the pentagons.

16 Trim the backing and batting to match the edges of the quilt top. Bind the quilt.

ELDERBERRY TEMPLATES

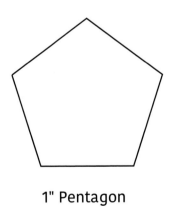

1" Pentagon

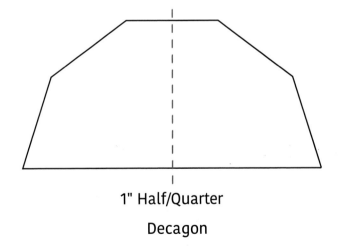

1" Half/Quarter
Decagon

CORNFLOWER

Cornflowers are a bright blue flower (a colour I could hardly find in my stash!) with an explosion of petals, so I wanted this quilt to have that same feeling of movement. Cornflower was my favourite quilt to make for this book, because it involved so much stitching pretty colours together, rather than lots of planning or precise cutting. For both the panel and the quilt, I chose light – medium prints for the scrappy sections so that the darker borders could contrast with them.

Panel Size – 10 ½" x 53"
Finished Quilt Size: 58" x 58"

CORNFLOWER BLOCK

1 Take an octagon and a petal, place right sides together and stitch along the ¾" sides.

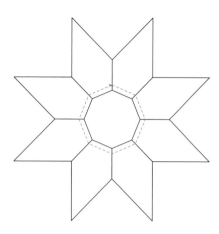

2 Sew a petal to each side of the octagon.

3 Sew between the petals.

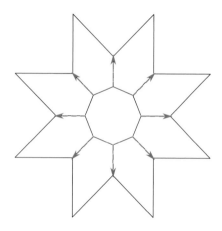

4 Sew a square between each petal.

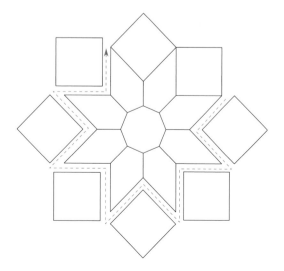

5 Sew a diamond between each square.

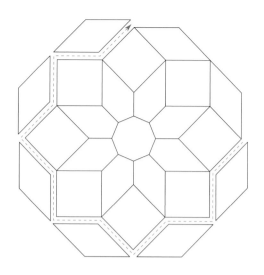

84

CORNFLOWER PANEL

PANEL SIZE 10 ½" x 53"

SHAPE REQUIREMENTS

- (5) ¾" Octagons
- (40) 2" Petals (measured along the long edge)
- (40) 2" Squares
- (40) 2" 8-point Diamonds
- (8) 4" Half Square Triangles
- (4) 4" Quarter Square Triangles

FABRIC REQUIREMENTS

OCTAGONS

(5) 2 ½" squares

PETALS

(40) scraps measuring at least 2 ½" x 3 ½"

SQUARES

¼ yard fabric (made up for 5 different prints.)

8-POINT DIAMONDS

¼ yard

EDGE TRIANGLES

¼ yard

CUTTING

Cut a ⅜" seam allowance around Petals.

SQUARES

(5) 22" x 2 ¾" strips, recut into (8) 2 ¾" squares per strip.

8-POINT DIAMONDS

(3) 2 ¼" x WOF strips. Recut a ⅜" seam allowance around the Diamonds. (14 per strip)

EDGE TRIANGLES

Cut (1) 3 ½" x WOF strip. Recut a ⅜" seam allowance around the Half Square Triangles.

Cut (1) 2 ¾" x WOF strip. Recut a ⅜" seam allowance around the Quarter Square Triangles.

INSTRUCTIONS

1 Make 5 Cornflower blocks.

2 Layout the blocks in a pleasing manner.

3 Sew the blocks together, in a row.

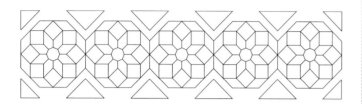

4 Fill in the gaps between them (top and bottom) with the HSTs. Sew a QST to the corners.

5 Take the papers out and press. Press the seams out at the top and bottom and sides of the row.

6 Trim ¼" from where the papers have been.

7 Sew a 2" x 10 ¼" rectangle to each end of the panel.

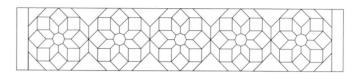

CORNFLOWER QUILT

FINISHED QUILT SIZE 58" x 58"

SHAPE REQUIREMENTS

CORNFLOWER BLOCKS AND STAR BLOCKS

- (36) ¾" Octagons
- (288) 2" Petals (measured along the long edge)
- (288) 2" Squares
- (288) 2" 8-point Diamonds
- (288) 1 ³⁄₁₆" 8-point Diamonds
- (116) 1 ³⁄₁₆" Squares
- (176) 1 ³⁄₁₆" Half Square Triangles

FABRIC REQUIREMENTS

- (36) Scraps at least 2 ½" square for Octagons
- (288) scraps at least 2 ⅛" x 3 ½" for Petals (or 20 fat 16ths)
- (18) Fat 8ths for Cornflower Squares.
- 1 ⅓ yd background fabric (aqua) for Cornflower Diamonds
- (288) scraps at least 1 ¾" x 2 ¾" for the star block Diamonds (or 12 fat 16ths)
- ¾ yard background fabric (teal) for star blocks
- ⅔ yd for binding
- 4 yds for backing
- 66" x 66" batting

CUTTING

CORNFLOWER BLOCKS

OCTAGONS: Cut with a ⅜" seam allowance around paper templates.

PETALS: Cut with a ⅜" seam allowance around paper templates.

2" SQUARES: Cut (3) 2 ¾" x 21" strips from each F8 and recut into (16) 2 ¾" squares

2" DIAMONDS: Cut 2 ¼" x WOF strips, recut into for diamonds (14 per strip)

STAR BLOCKS

DIAMONDS: Cut with a ⅜" seam allowance around paper templates.

SQUARES: Cut (6) 2" x WOF strips. Recut to (116) 2" squares.

TRIANGLES: Cut (7) 1 ½" x WOF strips. Place a triangle on the strip with the longest edge at the base. Cut a ⅜" seam allowance on each top side. Flip the next triangle and place it in the point of the fabric strip, with a ⅜" seam allowance. Cut a ⅜" seam allowance on the right edge. Continue cutting (176) triangles this way.

INSTRUCTIONS

1 Prepare all the pieces by basting the fabric to the paper templates.

2 Make 36 Cornflower blocks.

SEWING THE STAR BLOCKS

3 Take 8 of the smaller diamonds and lay them out to form a star.

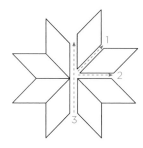

4 First, sew the diamonds into pairs. Then, sew the pairs into half-stars and then sew the halves into stars.

5 Then stitch the smaller squares and triangles around the outside of the star, alternating the squares and triangles.

6 Make 25 star blocks.

SEWING THE PARTIAL STAR BLOCKS

7 Just as you sewed the star blocks, make half-star blocks using 4 diamonds, 4 triangles and 1 square.

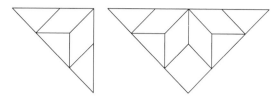

8 Make 20 half-star blocks.

9 Make quarter-star blocks in a similar way, using 2 diamonds and 3 triangles.

10 Make 4 quarter-star blocks.

ASSEMBLING THE QUILT TOP

11 Lay out the quilt blocks in rows to check for balanced colour placement as shown in diagram 11.

12 Snap a photo to remember the layout.

13 Sew the Cornflower blocks into rows of 6.

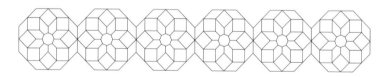

14 Fill the gaps above the top row with Quarter stars in the corners and half stars along the top.

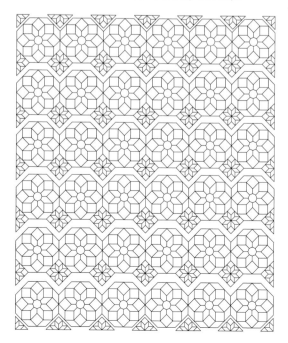

15 Fill the gaps below each of the first 5 rows with star blocks and each end with half star blocks.

16 Fill the gaps below the bottom row with quarter stars in the corners and half stars along the bottom.

17 Sew the rows together to complete your quilt top.

18 Take the papers out and press. Press the seams out at the top and bottom and sides of the quilt top.

19 Trim the quilt top at the top, bottom and sides, a ¼" from where the papers have been.

20 Layer the quilt back, right side down, batting and quilt top, right side up, and baste. Quilt as desired. I hand quilted Cornflower with diagonal lines through outer shapes of each Cornflower block.

21 Trim the backing and batting to match the edges of the quilt top. Bind the quilt.

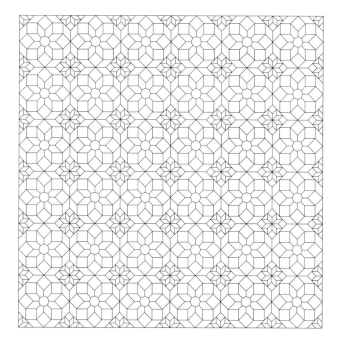

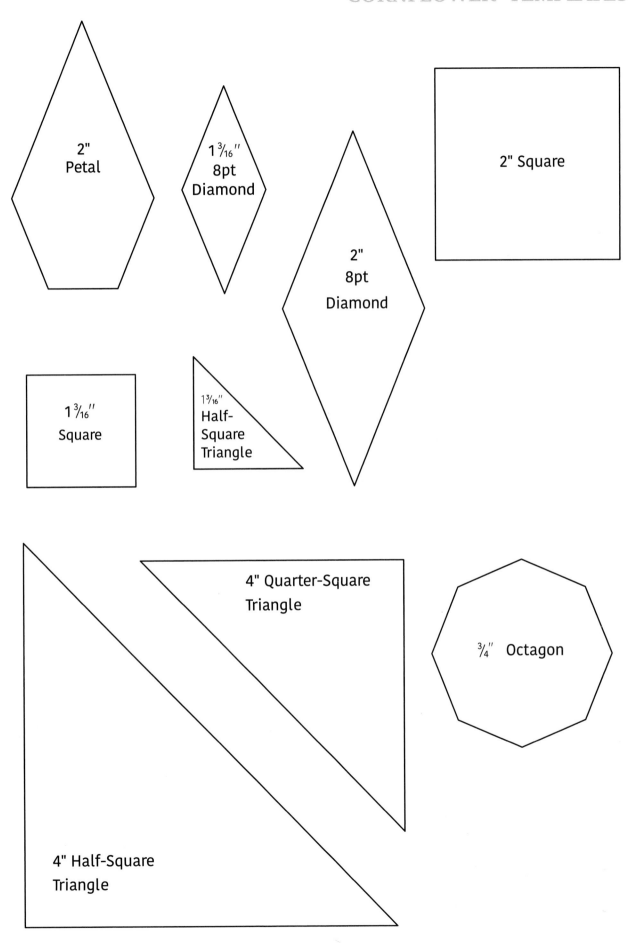

2"
Petal

$1\frac{3}{16}''$
8pt
Diamond

2"
8pt
Diamond

2" Square

$1\frac{3}{16}''$
Square

$1\frac{3}{16}''$
Half-
Square
Triangle

4" Quarter-Square
Triangle

$\frac{3}{4}''$ Octagon

4" Half-Square
Triangle

ROSEMARY

I have so many beautiful, big florals in my stash that I rarely use because I don't want to cut them up into tiny pieces! This quilt was designed for them. The spikey little Rosemary leaves are scattered throughout the quilt just occasionally to contrast with the gentle fabrics.

Panel Size - 10 ½" x 59 3/4"
Quilt size: 50" x 54"

ROSEMARY BLOCK

1 Place two 10-point diamonds right sides together and sew down one side. Without breaking the thread, place a third diamond over one of the sewn diamonds and stitch along the adjacent side.

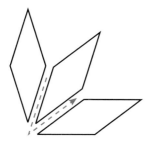

2 Sew two more 10-point diamonds together down one side. Without breaking the thread, place the three stitched diamonds over the sewn pair and stitch up the adjacent side.

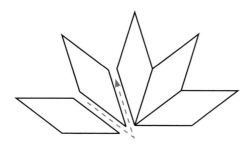

3 Sew (4) 5 point-diamonds in the gaps between the 10-point diamonds.

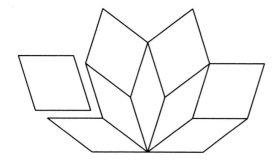

4 Remove the papers and press all the seams flat as they were, except for the bottom of the flower, which needs the seams pressed out. There will be tails left at the top of the diamonds, but these can be tucked away during the applique step.

5 Trim the bottom of the flower ¼" from where the papers have been.

6 Take a white rectangle and fold in half along the centre vertical axis. Press and open back out to use as a guide. Line up the centre of the flower with the guide line, and the base of the flower with the bottom of the rectangle. Pin or glue in place.

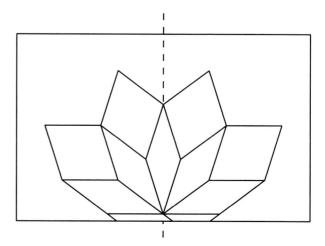

7 Applique the flower to the rectangle.

ROSEMARY PANEL

PANEL SIZE 10 ½" x 59 ¾"

SHAPE REQUIREMENTS
- (40) 2" 10-point Diamonds
- (32) 2" 5-point Diamonds

FABRIC REQUIREMENTS
- ½ yard white background fabric
- (3) fat 16ths for remaining rectangles (1 background and 2 feature prints)
- 2" x 16" rectangles for low volume diamonds.
- (32) scraps at least 2 ¾" x 3 ½"

CUTTING

WHITE BACKGROUNDS
(2) 6 ½" x WOF strips. Recut to (7) 6 ½" x 10 ½" rectangles.

COLOURED BACKGROUND
Trim (1) fat 16th to 6 ½" x 10 ½"
Feature prints: Trim the remaining fat 16ths to (1) 6 ½" x 10 ½" and (1) 5 ¾" x 10 ½"

10-POINT DIAMONDS
(8) 2" x 16" strips. Recut a ⅜" seam allowance around the diamonds. (5 per strip)

5-POINT DIAMONDS
Cut a ⅜" seam allowance around the paper templates.

INSTRUCTIONS

1 Prepare all the shapes by basting the fabric to the paper templates.

2 Make 8 Rosemary blocks on 7 white backgrounds and 1 coloured background.

3 Take your Rosemary blocks and the 2 feature prints and arrange in a column in a pleasing manner.

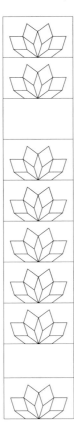

4 Starting at the bottom, sew the blocks together. Press.

ROSEMARY QUILT

The Rosemary quilt is made of 45 blocks – 9 Rosemary blocks and 36 patterned fabric blocks.

QUILT SIZE 50" x 54"

SHAPE REQUIREMENTS

🔶 (45) 2" 10 point-Diamonds

🔶 (36) 2" 5 point-Diamonds

FABRIC REQUIREMENTS

🔶 (36) fat 8ths in various prints.

🔶 ⅔ yd of white background fabric

CUTTING

WHITE BACKGROUNDS

(3) 6 ½" x WOF strips. Recut to (9) 6 ½" x 10 ½" rectangles.

FEATURE PRINTS

Cut (36) 6 ½" x 10 ½" rectangles from the fat 8ths. Save leftovers for diamonds.

10-POINT DIAMONDS

(9) 2" x 16" strips. Recut a ⅜" seam allowance around the diamonds. (5 per strip)

5-POINT DIAMONDS

(9) 2 ¾" x 13" Cut a ⅜" seam allowance around the paper templates. (4 per strip)

INSTRUCTIONS

1 Prepare all the shapes by basting the fabric to the paper templates.

2 Make 9 Rosemary blocks.

3 Take your Rosemary blocks and the 36 feature print blocks and arrange in a pleasing layout of 5 columns of 9 blocks.

4 Sew the blocks in the columns together.

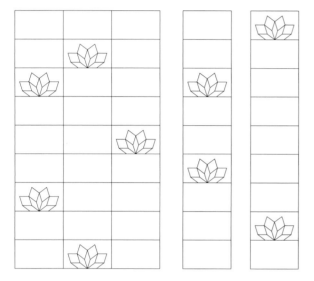

5 Sew the columns together.

6 Layer the quilt back, right side down, batting and quilt top, right side up, and baste. Quilt as desired. I hand quilted the Rosemary quilt – I outlined each Rosemary block and then worked diagonal lines through the other blocks from corner to corner.

7 Trim the backing and batting to match the edges of the quilt top. Bind the quilt.

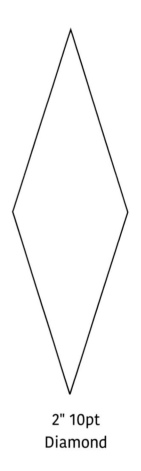

2" 10pt
Diamond

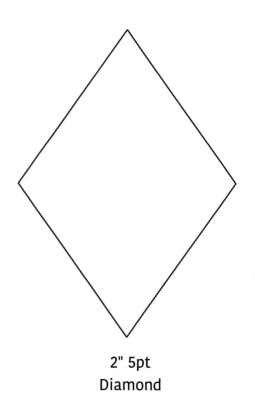

2" 5pt
Diamond

LAVENDER

Rather than your typical floral design, I wanted to make a quilt that gave the same, happy feeling of upward movement that Lavender flowers evoke. I love that it works with both a completely scrappy mix of fabrics, and a 2-3 colour palette!

Panel Size - 8 ¼" x 59"
Finished Quilt Size: 54" x 54"

LAVENDER BLOCK

1 Place 3 half hexagons around a triangle with the long sides touching the triangle.

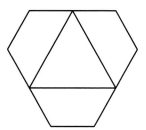

2 Stitch in place.

LAVENDER PANEL

PANEL SIZE 8 ¼" x 59"

SHAPE REQUIREMENTS

- (50) 3" Equilateral Triangles
- (77) 1 ½" Half Hexagons
- (25) 1 ½" Equilateral Triangles
- (2) 1 ½" Quarter Hexagons
- (4) 3" Half Triangles
- (2) 1 ½" Half Triangles

FABRIC REQUIREMENTS

- (54) scraps at least 3" x 3 ½"
- ½ yard low volume fabric
- ⅛ yard solid colour fabric

CUTTING

3" Triangles and Half Triangles: Cut a ⅜" seam allowance around the paper shapes. (Note: Half Triangles are directional! Cut and baste 2 facing left and 2 facing right.)

Half Hexagons and Quarter Hexagons: Cut (6) 2" x WOF strips from low volume fabric. Recut a ⅜" seam allowance around the paper shapes. (Note: Quarter Hexagons are directional! Cut and baste 1 facing left and 1 facing right.)

1 ½" Triangles and Half Triangles: Cut a 2" x WOF strip from solid colour fabric. Recut a ⅜" seam allowance around the paper shapes. (Note: Half Triangles are directional! Cut and baste 1 facing left and 1 facing right.)

INSTRUCTIONS

1 Prepare all the shapes by basting the fabric to the paper templates.

2 Make 25 Lavender Blocks.

3 Sew a half hexagon and quarter hexagon to a left facing half triangle and a right facing half triangle.

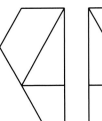

4 Stitch a small, solid colour triangle upside down to the top right of a Lavender block. Without breaking the thread, stitch a large triangle to the bottom right of the block. Repeat with 24 total Lavender blocks.

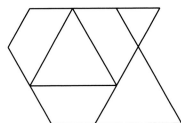

5 Stitch 12 blocks together into the top row. Finish with the Lavender Block without extra triangles. Sew small half triangles to the top corners of the row, and large half triangles to the bottom corners of the row.

6 Stitch a small triangle and a large triangle to the right side of the left half block.

7 Stitch 12 blocks together into the bottom row. Place the left half block on the left and the right half block on the right of the row.

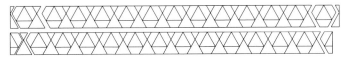
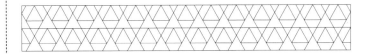

8 Stitch the top and bottom rows together.

9 Remove papers and press. Trim around the panel ¼" from where the papers have been.

LAVENDER QUILT

FINISHED QUILT Size 54" x 54"

SHAPE REQUIREMENTS
- (91) 4" Equilateral Triangles
- (143) 2" Half Hexagons
- (46) 2" Equilateral Triangles
- (8) 2" Quarter Hexagons
- (14) 4" Half Triangles
- (6) 2" Half Triangles

FABRIC REQUIREMENTS
- 3 ¼ yds Art Gallery Pure Elements in Honey
- 1 yard Art Gallery Pure Elements in Snow
- 52 scraps at least 2 ¾" square
- ½ yard for binding
- 4 yards for backing
- 62" x 62" batting

CUTTING

4" EQUILATERAL TRIANGLES
(7) 4 ⅜" x WOF strips. Cut ⅜" seam allowance around the first template from one end of a strip. Cut around the second template by flipping the shape upside down and placing it in the angle left by the first cut. Cut the remaining triangles in the same manner.

HALF HEXAGONS
(13) 2 ⅜" x WOF strips of Honey fabric. Cut ⅜" seam allowance around the first template from one end of a strip. Cut around the second template by flipping the shape upside down and placing it in the angle left by the first cut. Cut the remaining half hexagons in the same manner.

2" EQUILATERAL TRIANGLES
Cut a ⅜" seam allowance around the paper templates from scraps.

QUARTER HEXAGONS
(1) 2 ½" x WOF strip. Cut a ⅜" seam allowance around the paper templates. (Note: Quarter Hexagons are directional! Cut and baste 4 facing left and 4 facing right.)

4" HALF TRIANGLES
Cut a ⅜" seam allowance around the paper templates from remaining white fabric. (Note: Half Triangles are directional! Cut and baste 7 facing left and 7 facing right.)

2" HALF TRIANGLES
Cut a ⅜" seam allowance around the paper templates from scraps. (Note: Half Triangles are directional! Cut and baste 3 facing left and 3 facing right.)

BORDERS
(2) 7 ½" x WOF
(1) 16" x WOF
(1) 24" x WOF
(1) 24" square

INSTRUCTIONS

1 Prepare all the shapes by basting the fabric to the paper templates.

2 Make 45 Lavender blocks.

3 Make a (4) half blocks facing right and a (4) half blocks facing left.

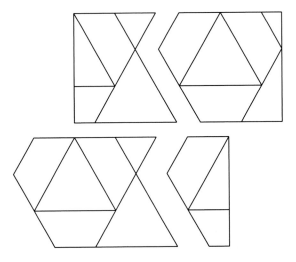

4 Stitch a small, colour triangle upside down to the top right of a Lavender block. Without breaking the thread, stitch a large white triangle to the bottom right of the block. Repeat with 42 total Lavender blocks.

5 To the 3 remaining Lavender Blocks, stitch a small, colour half triangle upside down to the top right. Without breaking the thread, stitch a large, white, half triangle to the bottom right of the block. These should make a straight edge on the right-hand side of the block.

6 Stitch a small, colour triangle upside down to the top right of a left-side half block. Without breaking the thread, stitch a large white triangle to the bottom right of the block. Repeat with all left side half blocks.

7 The quilt is made of (4) row A's and (3) row B's.

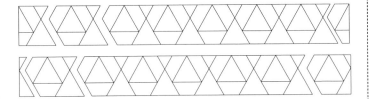

8 Row A: Begin with a left-side half block, then line up 6 complete blocks. Finish with a right-side half block.

9 Row B: Stitch a small, colour half triangle to the top, left side of a Lavender Block. Continue down the bottom, left side with a large, white half triangle. Add (5) more Lavender blocks to the row. Finish with a Lavender block with half triangles on the right side.

10 Lay the rows out A, B, A, B, A, B, A from top to bottom. Sew the rows together.

11 Trim the quilt top a ¼" from where the papers have been.

12 Line up the end of one of the 7 ½" border strips with the edge of the quilt top and machine sew the border to the bottom. Press. Trim the strip in line with the edge of the quilt top.

13 Line up the end of the other 7 ½" border strip with the bottom left edge of the quilt top and machine sew the border to the left side. Press. Trim the strip in line with the edge of the quilt top.

14 Line up the end of the 16" border strip with the bottom right edge of the quilt top and machine sew the border to the right side. Press. Trim the strip in line with the edge of the quilt top.

15 Sew the 24" border strip and the 24" square along one short edge and press. Line up the end of this strip with the top left edge of the quilt top and machine sew the borders to the top of the quilt. Press and trim any excess.

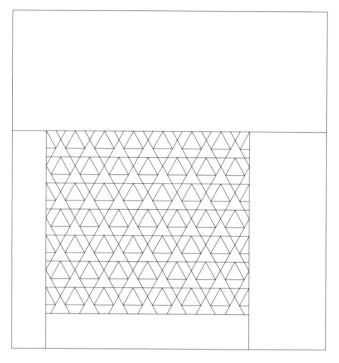

16 Layer the quilt back, right side down, batting and quilt top, right side up, and baste. Quilt as desired. I machine quilted Lavender with horizontal lines approximately 1 ½" apart.

17 Trim the backing and batting to match the edges of the quilt top. Bind the quilt.

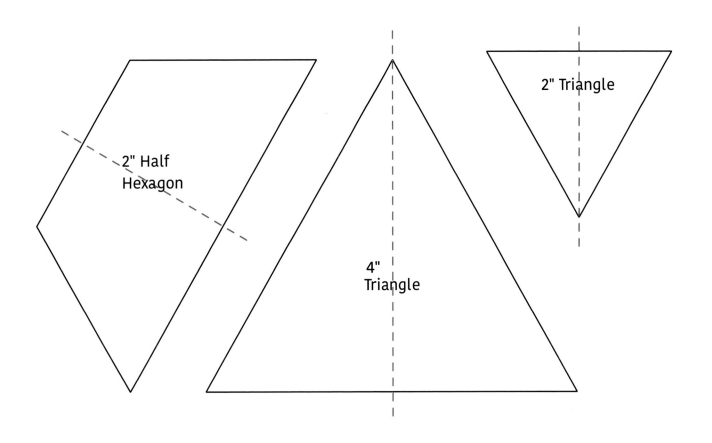

2" Half
Hexagon

4"
Triangle

2" Triangle

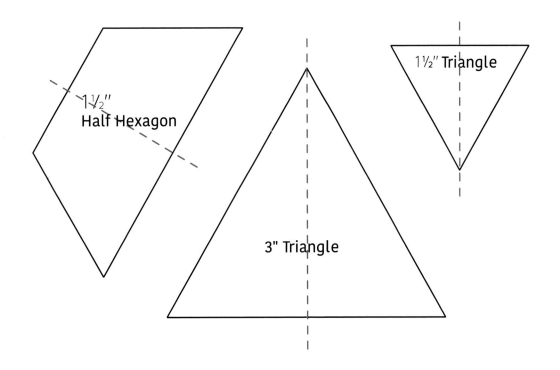

1½"
Half Hexagon

3" Triangle

1½" Triangle